T0097933

If My People…

God's Answer for America's Troubles

PAUL JAMES CASTEEL, SR.

ACKNOWLEDGEMENT

* * * *

I believe this book was inspired by the Holy Spirit. I thank Him for it and give Him full credit.

Even though He inspires, He does not vocally speak each word that is to be written. I have made quite a few revisions to what I originally wrote, thinking that something could be stated better.

Along that line there are those who have made suggestions that have made this book better and more readable than what it would have been if not for them. I want to thank my wife Diane, my pastor friend Gary Hines, and Jeff Daly, founder and director of National Day of Repentance. They read the original draft and their suggestions helped me complete the final draft.

Later on, I read a book Jeff gave me entitled "River and Streams in the Desert". Even though the manuscript was completed, I found scriptures in his book that were relevant to my purpose in writing "If My People". I went back and made some more revisions.

I have two friends who graciously took it on themselves to take this book, chapter by chapter, and make suggestions to improve my grammar and the word flow. This was unexpected and is greatly appreciated. Marge Thies and Rene Abreu, thank you. You are great friends.

Barbara Reincke suggested some scriptures which I used and later my friend Fred Brown made some suggested corrections which hadn't been caught in the transcript I gave him.

Thank you all for your contributions to improve this book and for encouraging me.

TABLE OF CONTENTS

INTRODUCTION

As I begin this writing, it is July 4, 2017, two hundred forty one years after the signing of the Declaration of Independence.

Before I began my day, I felt that I should thank God for this country. As I did so, I was inspired to write about how the Old Testament verse of 2 Chronicles 7:14 (written to the Jews) relates to America today – to Jew and Gentile alike. I have written about this scripture in a short, informal way as a layman and sent it to friends, family, and others on mailing lists that I was a part of in the past.

I believe thousands of frustrated Christians across America need to understand how this scripture relates to our great country in our time of turmoil thousands of years after it was written. More importantly, I think they would like to know what they can do personally as individuals in the body of Christ throughout America to replace the Godlessness that permeates this great nation - to a depth that we might not even understand - with a renewed God-fearing lifeblood. God gave us the answer in this one simply stated, self-explanatory scripture. Unfortunately, it has been overlooked by many devoted Christians as pertaining only to the Jewish nation long ago. And to some of us who have seen that it actually is relevant to America today, it has been acknowledged only in part.

I believe it is important to get the full, unadulterated message out to all Christians because politicians cannot plot the best course for the future of our children and grandchildren. The state of our Union today is ample proof of the truth of this statement. As political differences abound and grow, Godlessness increases. Any adult over forty years old can attest to this. Those of us who are now senior citizens stand amazed at the unbelievable rate of spiritual decline we have seen in just our lifetimes in this great nation.

Only by the hand of God will this be reversed and only when we Christians do as God requires. Then He will do it Himself, possibly through the hands of those in power, very probably in a way that we could never imagine. Either way it will not be by human genius or power. We have seen how human genius and power have only taken us farther down a very dark path that is getting darker and darker very rapidly.

We like to talk about how much progress science and technology have made in the last century, which is true in their own realm. On the other hand immorality, godlessness, and crime have increased dramatically. The only light at the end of the tunnel is that which can come only from the Creator. We must remember that in the end, the Creator is also a destroyer of all that is ungodly.

If we do not honor God as He desires and requires, a great future for our kids will not be accomplished and we will go the path of many powerful nations before us. We do not want to believe this could happen to so great a nation – our nation - but God is not a respecter of persons or nations. People, specifically Christians, must respect and honor Him if we want to see this nation turned around. To continue to survive and thrive, our nation must be upheld not only in prayer but by more individual submission to our great Creator by Christian men and women who truly love God and want to serve Him. We will see through scripture that praying for our country is not enough. It's important, but only the beginning.

The men who signed the Declaration of Independence were flawed, as all of us are. They made mistakes but many of them were men of God. They prayed and sought His guidance. Because of these men and many God fearing men and women since then, we live in a great nation, the greatest nation ever. We have experienced God's favor for a long time. I wouldn't want to live anywhere else. We are beginning to see some of these men discredited today but we need to remember that God has used flawed men for His purposes throughout history. Even the great prophets and apostles were not without fault. But God used them and we still read about them and their exploits in the Bible today. They cannot be removed from history.

A lot has been said and written about the spiritual decline of America over the last few years by some truly faithful Christian leaders as well as lay people. This is written not in an attempt to overshadow them, but to supplement their teaching in an effort to bring this subject to the forefront for those who may not have read or heard it before and to further validate the need for Christians to follow the word of God as it pertains to the USA. The future of America is in the hands of God whether the politicians or the general public believe it or not. 2 Chronicles 7:14 describes in detail how we Christians can open the door for God to do what He wants to do for us, His people, today. He wants a bright future for us and our children and grandchildren, but we have to be in a position to receive it. He will not force it on us or continue to bless us as this nation gets farther and farther out of His will, putting Him behind all other things deemed more important by an ungodly world and even some religious people.

In the pages that follow my emphasis will be on what we Christians must do to see America make an about face. When I say the future of all of America is in the hands of Christians, it may sound like I'm saying all Christians are neglecting their duties as Christians. I know that is not the case. Many of you have done and will do much more than I have for the kingdom of God and America. Please understand that I am saying many, maybe most, of us have not put our backs to the plow and done our part, including myself. We could all do more to lift our great country out of the mire we're getting sucked into. I don't know why of all people God has given the following pages to me to share in this way. I am no more than a messenger, a tool to expand the understanding of this scripture. When I say the future of America is in the hands of us Christians, I know that it is truly in God's hands, but we are His tools to do His will.

I will forewarn you: this book is not "politically or socially correct" as some deem necessary in today's world. I will not mince words. We have had too much of that. Some will think I'm being judgmental, but my purpose is not to judge. It is to shine a light on what God has said is necessary for a nation to thrive and even to just survive. One cannot fully speak truth without saying things that will offend some. Nevertheless, I will attempt to speak truth, the whole truth, and nothing but the truth. For those who think I'm pointing fingers, please be open to the scriptures themselves and let them speak to you. After all, scripture is the Word of God and there is no other Truth that can save us.

My purpose is not to please everyone, but to encourage all Christians to look beyond what seems right to us as limited human beings and look to the Almighty God who alone has the power to make us a greater nation than we are now, greater even than we ever have been. This is the same God who started a great work over 200 yrs. ago in a new, floundering country.

This is written for those who believe that we are going down the wrong path and want to see us do an "about face" to move in a positive way for the good of our nation and the glory of God; for those who are open to the possibility that God's word, specifically 2 Chronicles 7:14, is the one and only key to a grand future for this country; AND who are willing to personally submit to the mighty hand of God in fulfilling this scripture in himself or herself for the glory of God and the benefit of our posterity, our children and grandchildren, for many generations to come. Acting on the belief in a scripture is more important than just mentally believing that it is true. This is a true case where actions speak louder than words.

Even some Christians may not accept the fact that we as a body of believers have become complacent and have fallen into Satan's trap of making us think everything is going to be OK in the long run. But I personally believe that if this nation does not turn back to God, the not too distant future of America will be dismal.

Politicians can make all the promises they want but neither they nor their promises are the answer to what we need to survive as a world-class power and especially as a nation "under God". I don't mean to be melodramatic and I'm not a doomsayer or a pessimist. I am a Christian and a realist that understands my responsibility to this nation and our posterity. I hope that you will consider, agree with, and act on what is written in the following pages as supported by the Word of God. As I said, this is a great nation. But it could be greater.

One of Abraham Lincoln's supposed quotes is, "America will never be destroyed from the outside. If we falter and lose our freedoms, it will be because we destroyed ourselves." Whether he actually said it or not, it is something we need to think about very seriously.

Many years later, Nikita Khrushchev, premier of the Soviet Union from 1958 to 1964 said, "We do not have to invade the United States, we will destroy you from within." Khrushchev lost power and is now dead, but what he said should make us shudder because it is still a possibility that we may be our own worst enemy.

One of our greatest leaders and one of our greatest enemies both said basically the same thing concerning the future of the good old USA.

I hope this book will encourage others like me with the understanding that God wants to speak to us and guide us in a quest for a better America through spiritual maturity when we are open to Him. I pray that you will see my desire for each of you and this nation and join me in my journey on the road to spiritual maturity which, if traveled by enough of us, will lead to the healing of this nation. Just think: you, me, and our Christian brothers and sisters and no-one else must be the catalyst in restoring America to a country with which God is pleased and will bless once again.

I have prayed and will continue to pray that this book will be seen as God's wishes for the United States of America given to and written by an imperfect human being who loves the Lord and wants only the best for our great nation. I pray that each scripture be understood and taken to heart by each reader and that if I have personally said anything that someone may question that their full attention be given to scripture itself.

As stated earlier, I started this book in 2017. In 2018 I started another book which I am still working on and set this one aside until this year, 2019. This year I have edited most of my 2017 writing and added additional thoughts God has given me, completing the book. You will see a few notes where it was necessary to explain the 2019 addition because of the difference in time and what has occurred since I began.

As you read this, events noted are in the past. They are history. The things we see in the news today are in different places and they have different characters. But the issues are the same, only worse. Each day has a new story of immorality and ungodliness. Many of our government agencies and even churches are succumbing to the evil influences of the devil. It is a spiritual war carried out by mankind.

No matter what year you are reading this, it's going to be worse than the year before if we Christians do not submit to the authority and direction of God.

CHAPTER 1

Will History Repeat Itself?

★ ★ ★ ★

It has been said in various ways that if we ignore history, it will repeat itself. History itself proves this to be true. Throughout the ages nations have risen and fallen in different ways. Think about this: up until the day the USA became the most powerful nation in the world, every single nation, without exception, which had at one time been *number one*, had fallen from the glory it once knew; some even being totally destroyed. And I bet not a single one of them thought at the height of their power a greater nation would replace them, much less defeat them in war, as has been true of some.

Are we immune to failure? I think not. No nation is too big, too powerful, or too good to fall. Unfortunately, that includes our good old USA.

Don't get me wrong. I love this country and I'm not putting it down. Rather, I'm ringing the bell for us to get back in the ring and win the victory over the forces that are pulling us down. We cannot hide our heads in the sand. I am a proud American and thank God I was born in the land of the free and the home of the brave. I'm proud of the men and women that have served for over 200 years to make us what we are today, friends, family, and those I never knew, 10's of thousands of whom gave their lives for those who would come after them, including you and me. I don't want us to give up even a little bit of what they provided for us through their sacrifices.

As I'm looking back over this on November 12, 2017, Veterans' day was yesterday. Last Sunday I visited a church some friends attend. At the beginning of the service they had veterans from every branch of service come forward so we might honor them. I stood in awe of them. I pray to God that these and many others did not serve in vain.

What does it take to be *numero uno*? Bloomberg recently ranked America as # 28 of great nations, partly due to health problems, violence, substance abuse, and the suicide rate. Other studies show similar results where we're falling behind in infrastructure and education. We are no longer looked up to and respected by many nations. (And all of this at a time when some even say we are no longer a Christian nation.)

Whether we believe the rankings or not, we have to understand we aren't where we were when my parents (the Greatest Generation, as Tom Brokaw called them, and with which I wholeheartedly agree) including my dad were in their prime, serving this nation in various ways during WW II. Many of those who did not go to war, including my mom, served in factories and farms to support those who were overseas, some of whom never returned home. When the war was over, those who had survived came together and greatly contributed to the abundance this great nation has today. My parents, aunts, and uncles, all of whom are gone now, were in that generation and I thank God for them with a lump in my throat.

Of course there are also claims stating we are still the greatest country in the world and I and many others still believe we are. I know there are areas where we still excel compared to other countries. I don't dispute that, but I'm looking forward to a time when we excel in even more areas; when we are once again respected and even loved because of who we are; and most importantly, Whom we serve. I look forward to the US once again being called a Christian nation, a nation under God whose people fear, honor, respect, and love Him.

inserted March 9, 2019:

Today's news pits Democrats against Republicans. But let me tell you, ladies and gentlemen, politics and all the agendas supported by rival groups are nothing but a smoke-screen to hide the real battle that is waging not only here in America, but throughout the world. In the grand scheme of things it matters not whether you are Democrat, Republican, Independent, or whatever label may be hung on you or what label you proudly display. Politics, politicians, and many of their agendas are nothing more than tools used by the father of lies to hide the real battle that is going on all around us.

It is time to take off the labels and submit to God alone in every aspect of our lives. I'm not saying we should stick our head in the sand, become pacifists, ignore what's going on, and let God just "do His thing". He will do His thing, but we will see in 2 Chronicles 7:14 that we can influence what that thing will be. Neither am I saying the destruction of the America we love is inevitable.

None of us are exempt from our future. At the age of 71, I doubt I will see the full downfall of America if it does happen. But if we don't open our eyes and hearts, my children and grandchildren may very well experience a great tragedy, much greater even than 911, and so may yours.

In saying this, I in no way minimize that terrible event that killed so many thousands of innocent Americans and negatively affected many more. If I am accused of that or any other supposed act or thought against my great country, the accuser will be participating in the smoke-screen that is hiding the real truth about what we Americans are up against. When I say it will be greater, I'm speaking of the magnitude. Rather than thousands being affected, tens and even hundreds of thousands will see their lives dramatically changed; and not in a way they desire.

Almost 2,000 years ago the apostle Paul wrote in Ephesians 6:12, "<u>For we wrestle not against flesh and blood, but against prin-cipalities, against powers, against the rulers of the darkness of this world, against spiritual wickedness in high places.</u>" Paul had no idea what would be going on today. I think he actually believed the second coming would have taken place well before now and there wouldn't even be a "today" as we know it.

But his words, inspired by the Holy Spirit, are as true today as they were way back then. We can blame the politicians, current or past presidents, or any individual or group we want to. But those who did wrong were (and are) no more than tools used by the most powerful schemer of all time. You know who I'm talking about. Call him Lucifer, Satan, or the devil. He is real, alive, and walking throughout this nation to see who he can devour. And if we who fear and love God don't do as He implores us, it could be our own precious children and grandchildren who are led astray, even though we may think, "That couldn't happen to my kids". It can! It may have happened to your friends' kids and they too thought it couldn't.

These words may turn some of you off right now. But if it does you need to open your eyes and look around. We protest, ridicule, and put people in jail for torturing or killing animals. We call them monsters; we roast them in news broadcasts; and they have their lives threatened. And yet we have almost totally banned capital punishment for the heartless murderers and rapists who destroy and wreak havoc in human lives because it is "cruel and unusual punishment". When they receive long sentences or even life in prison, they will probably get out early.

At the same time we have made it legal to kill unborn human babies because the mother "has her own rights".

As I insert this in March, 2019, in the last few weeks politicians in two states have been talking about making it legal to kill a baby – or making it comfortable until it dies even after it has been born. Folks, when a human sperm fertilizes a human egg, the immediate result is a human being. It is not an animal or a "thing" that will only be considered human after a certain amount of time deemed by man for it to be so. That tiny fertilized egg has everything in it to become a grown man or woman if allowed to. That tiny human being is made in the image of God. We have stooped to a very low position when we say it's OK to destroy it because the mother has her own rights. It is not up to man to decide who will live or die. Abortion of a human fetus no matter how much or little it has developed is nothing less than murder.

As I write these words, I am very aware there are children born who will never be "normal" as we consider normal and I'm not degrading these children in any way. There are occasions when the mother's health or life may be at risk. I have no comprehension of how terrible these situations are and don't pretend to have all the answers. I am really at a loss of words in these matters. But I do know that God rules. Life and death are His choice, not ours.

If you stop and look at our national situation from God's perspective, you must realize He won't put up with this much longer. Unless our dilemma is reversed we will go from abortion to infanticide; possibly to geriatric genocide. If you don't think so, do nothing and your grandchildren could very well see it. I don't imagine my grandparents had any idea in the early 1900's abortion would be accepted by so many people in this country they loved so dearly.

But as bad as it is, even this is just a symptom of something much deeper and sinister. Again, I'm not a doomsayer. I mention this to point out we "ain't where we oughta be". We need to be doom slayers.

I believe our many problems are obvious to most of us even though we may not want to believe it. We may even think our problems aren't really that bad and this great country can't follow in the steps of those great powers who fell before America was even thought about. My purpose is to encourage Christians everywhere to realize it is our responsibility to understand and follow scripture and do our part to make this nation once again the greatest nation in the world for all those that come after us. That is not an unrealistic goal if we each do some soul searching, reach deep down into our very being, and ask ourselves, "Am I doing my part or am I just going with the flow, thinking everything will be alright?"

Let it not be said that America fell under our watch.

Years ago we heard a lot about the "silent majority". This was in reference to the majority of good people not speaking up when they saw something wrong. The vocal minority got things done because they had an agenda while the silent majority sat around thinking the problems would just go away, or at least not get any worse. And how did that work out? I don't believe there's any thinking person who could honestly say the US is in a better place morally than it was 50 years ago. Aren't civilized nations supposed to be getting better and better as we learn from past experiences? We are becoming more advanced in technology without a doubt. But we are regressing morally and spiritually.

We Christians are today's silent majority. We may not even be a majority any longer. We have allowed our country to sink to a level of immorality our forefathers could never anticipate happening in this great land.

The following chapters discuss 2 Chronicles 7:14 which is part of God's directions to Solomon after he built and dedicated the temple. This verse, I believe, shows the only way to see the salvation of America – spiritually, economically, militarily, and in every other way. In verse 13 God had spoken about tragedies that could befall Israel. Then verse 14 reads, "*If my people, which are called by my name, shall humble themselves, and pray, and seek my face, and turn from their wicked ways; then will I hear from heaven, and will forgive their sin, and will heal their land*."

This is a four-fold directive from He who can do all things to we who desperately need help if we are to see our nation become even better and greater than it once was. A directive is sort of like an order to do something. In the strictest sense, this scripture is not an actual order. It gives mankind an option "to do or not to do". However, to a Christian who doesn't want to sit idly by while our nation continues to spiral down a very dark hole, it is more than an option. It is truly a directive for every Christian in America. It is a directive for YOU! Will you heed the call?

CHAPTER 2

If

★ ★ ★ ★

It has been said, "If" is the biggest word in the dictionary. "If" is the word we use when we reach a place where we are faced with a choice: If I do "this", what will happen? If I don't do "that", what will happen?

Yogi Berra has been credited with saying, "When you come to a fork in the road, take it". Folks, we in America are at a "fork in the road". As Christians we have a decision to make. Are we going to take the easy road, the broad way, and let things go on with a que sera sera attitude / whatever will be will be, or are we going to take the hard road, the narrow way, and follow God, letting Him save and restore our nation? The choice is ours. The future of America rests on our shoulders, not on those of the politicians.

We Christians grab hold of God's promises and claim them for our own. But we often overlook the fact that many, maybe most of His promises are conditional. They are conditional in the fact that something must happen before the promise is fulfilled. That "something" is very often what we must do ourselves. But we often are not willing to perform our part of the arrangement, or at least we will go only so far. Yet we still expect God to do His part and give us His promise.

After Jesus was raised from the dead He said "--*All power is given unto me in heaven and in earth*." Matthew 28:18b. The One who created heaven and earth determines who has power. Sometimes He allows people to come to power He doesn't really want as he did King Saul. Sometimes He appoints His choice as He did David. But in all cases, power is granted from above; it is also removed from above as King Saul found out.

All who have read the Bible have seen the afore-mentioned verse 14, but God uses another "if" five verses later while telling Solomon what he must do personally:

But if ye turn away, and forsake my statutes and my commandments, which I have set before you, and shall go and serve other gods, and worship them; Then will I pluck them up by the roots out of my land which I have given them; and this house, which I have sanctified for my name, will I cast out of my sight, and will make it to be a proverb and a byword among all nations. And this house, which is high, shall be an astonishment to every one that passeth by it; so that he shall say, Why hath the LORD done thus unto this land, and unto this house? And it shall be answered, Because they forsook the LORD God of their fathers, which brought them forth out of the land of Egypt, and laid hold on other gods, and worshipped them, and served them: therefore hath he brought all this evil upon them. 2 Chronicles 7: 19-22 (KJV)

Note God didn't list all the people's sins. Of all the things He could have accused them of, the only one He spoke of was turning away from God and worshipping idols. We will talk about this in the chapters ahead.

In verse 14 God told Solomon what He would do **for** the Israelites – *if* they did what He said. Then in vs. 19-22 above, He told him what He would do **to** them *if* Solomon took the other fork in the road. Solomon was king and if he disobeyed God, his subjects would follow as indicated in verse 22. We don't have a king, but many of our leaders have disobeyed God and the nation is following, whether by choice or by mandate of law.

One might say this was in the Old Testament; we are living in the New Testament so it doesn't apply to us today; a loving God wouldn't do that now. But I'm afraid He would. God does not change.

But why or how would it specifically apply to us in America today? We haven't forsaken God or his statutes and commandments, have we? Maybe we've become a little lax, but we certainly haven't forsaken Him have we? And we certainly don't serve and worship other gods, do we? We go to church; we support church projects and activities; and maybe even tithe and give to the poor. So how would 2 Chronicles 7:14 relate to us?

Folks, I'm not judging anyone. But even as Christians, we've fallen short in our personal relationships due to obligations to other things in our lives and we know it. Jesus said in Revelation 3:16, "_So then because thou art lukewarm, and neither cold nor hot, I will spue thee out of my mouth._" He also said in Matthew 6:24, _"No man can serve two masters: for either he will hate the one, and love the other; or else he will hold to the one, and despise the other. Ye cannot serve God and mammon._" These are not verses we should take lightly. I may think they do not apply to me. But do they?

Do we cling to our pleasures at the expense of our spiritual growth? When other things or people become more important to us than God, we have in actuality set Him aside. "Other gods" in America today would be anything or any person we have allowed to become more important to us than God Himself. He is patient and forgiving, but He will not accept second place forever. Sometimes actions do speak louder than words. What do our actions say about our love for God more than anything else, including our possessions, hobbies, occupations, and even family? When almost every decision we make is based on money, possessions, and the pleasures of the time being, we need to sit back and consider what God may be thinking of us because we may not be thinking much of Him.

A way of life

As we will see later, in verse 14 God is talking not just about a quick prayer, brief activity, sacrifice, or ceremony to undertake to save the Israelite nation, but about a personal relationship with His people that would affect the course of history. It's a way of living more than an occasional act that God is interested in. Good acts are important but they are the natural by-products of righteous living. Doing the "right things" does not bring righteousness.

I believe these verses are just as pertinent to us today as they were way back then. The apostle Paul said in Galatians 6:7, "*Be not deceived; God is not mocked: for whatsoever a man soweth, that shall he also reap.*" We each need to ask if we have personally mocked God in our religious lives. Is He first in our daily activities Sunday through Saturday, or do we include Him only when it's convenient or expected by our peers?

So what does a personal relationship with God have to do with the future of America? Everything according to scripture. The first three directives of verse 14 are that His people (us today) must humble ourselves, pray, and seek His face. That is how we build a relationship with our Lord and Savior.

Then it says we must turn from our wicked ways. We aren't wicked are we? Remember what Jesus said to one of his closest disciples, a pillar of the early church, one of those flawed men, in Matthew 16:23. *But he turned, and said unto Peter, Get thee behind me, Satan: thou art an offence unto me: for thou savourest not the things that be of God, but those that be of men.* This may sound too simplistic, but it all boils down to priorities. Our priorities must line up with His for individual spiritual growth followed by the moral and maybe even the physical salvation of our nation. Who or what is first in our lives? Who or what is first in your life? Do you believe the future of your loved ones is affected by your priorities?

God is more interested in the inner man than He is the land the man walks on. But the healing of the land will come as a byproduct of the healing of the inner man.

Isaiah 55:8, 9 says, *"For my thoughts are not your thoughts, neither are your ways my ways, saith the LORD. For as the heavens are higher than the earth, so are my ways higher than your ways, and my thoughts than your thoughts."* James 4:17 states, *"Therefore to him that knoweth to do good, and doeth it not, to him it is sin."* This says to me that as we go about our daily lives, we may be doing or saying things that seem perfectly good, honorable, and honest. But since God says His thoughts and ways are above mine, maybe we need to take a second or third look at how we live our lives.

Do we spend hours in recreation, other activities, or even in idleness that have no eternal benefit and only a few minutes, once in a while, with our Lord? I submit to you that in the eyes of God, this is sin. Sin is any act contrary to the will of God. It is not limited only to those obvious sins of murder, theft, and those other sins that would land us in jail. Any time I do something out of the will of God or don't do something that is in His will, I am sinning because I am replacing God with something else in my life. I am relegating my Creator to a place lower than the created things I enjoy or feel to be necessary.

Fortunately, He knows my many weaknesses and forgives me because I have received Christ as my Savior, ask for forgiveness, and repent when I know I have displeased Him. But He expects me to do better. If I don't, there will be consequences. God chastises those He loves, maybe for a brief time; maybe for 400 years for a nation as He did the Israelites; maybe forever.

Those of us in my generation and before received harsh consequences when we disobeyed our parents. Our folks loved us, but we
were disciplined sometimes in unpleasant and even painful ways
when we went astray. Sometimes it was in anger, but it was always to
make us understand we needed to repent of our ways and "straighten
up". After I grew up, I used to kid my mother about killing a peach
tree by breaking switches off. (Of course, I reminded her I really didn't
deserve the spankings.) God disciplines His children and He knows
who deserves punishment. He will either initiate punishment or allow
it. And He can't be fooled. He knows who deserves it. There is certainly
grace. But it sometimes follows a period of learning and maybe even
suffering, not only for we who have fallen, but also for those we love.

I must realize I not only live and breathe as a fleshly human being,
but also too often think in the flesh even though I'm a Christian, saved
by grace through the blood of Jesus. But God the Father, Son, and Holy
Spirit think in spiritual terms – ALWAYS! They are not bowed down
with fleshly desires. I know I can never fully be that way on this earth
because I'm human. But I can and do need to pray and seek His will
in my every-day life. The old saying, practice makes perfect applies
to the Christian walk. I would not dare say it is easy, but the more I
submit to God's thoughts and desires for myself, the more I will be
in line with His ways. Then I will begin to see some of the things I do
may not be morally or ethically wrong, but they are not His will for my
life or this country because they have replaced something grander in
the sight of God, Himself, and will be irrelevant in eternity. We don't
want to admit we have replaced God with our own desires. But if we
have, we must first admit it to ourselves and to God. We must then
repent of whatever it was making a 180 degree turn from it and to God.

IF we frail human beings will humble ourselves before God and
admit we haven't honored and served Him the way He desires – for
our own good; **IF** we will pray in His will; **IF** we will seek His face;

and **IF** we will turn from our own self-centered (wicked) ways, taking our eyes off ourselves and our desires, and put Him first in our lives, **THEN AND ONLY THEN** will He hear from heaven, forgive us of our sins, and heal our nation. I don't believe there is any other way that healing will take place. God has allowed this nation to survive initially and then to prosper for a long time, just as He did the Israelites when they started slipping morally. But after a while, He had enough and Israel fell. He allowed this to happen to His favored people. We cannot assume He will do any different to us thousands of years later.

God used a lot of "ifs" in the Bible. He was always giving options because He gave mankind a free will. We can do as we please but only to an extent. He explained what the consequences were by explaining what would happen "if ——". Too often, throughout history, God's people have ignored His warnings. I pray that will not be said of America a few decades down the road.

CHAPTER 3

My People, Which Are Called by My Name

★ ★ ★ ★

His ancient words are speaking to me today, and I hope to every reader of this book. They are as relevant now as they were thousands of years ago. Throughout the Old Testament the Jews were God's chosen people. After Christ was crucified and rose from the dead and before He ascended into heaven, Jesus told His disciples, *"...Go ye into all the world, and preach the gospel to every creature."* Mark 16:15. He was effectively telling them that the gospel was not for the Jews only. Then in Romans 2: 28,29 Paul said *"For he is not a Jew, which is one outwardly; neither is that circumcision, which is outward in the flesh: But he is a Jew, which is one inwardly; and circumcision is that of the heart, in the spirit, and not in the letter; whose praise is not of men, but of God."*

These first disciples taught that to personally receive Christ as Savior was the only way to become a Christian and spend eternity with God. And it wasn't for the Jewish people only. It was and is for all who will receive it. There is no other provision for salvation in the Bible. *And when he* (Barnabas) *had found him* (Paul)*, he brought him* *unto Antioch. And it came to pass, that a whole year they assembled themselves with the church, and taught much people. And the disciples were called Christians first in Antioch.* Acts 11:26.

The people may be different and the times certainly are different now, but God is not. Since you've stayed with me this long, He must be talking to you too. A Christian is one who has repented (turned away from his sins); asked Jesus Christ to forgive and save him; and committed his life to His Lordship.

It matters not what denomination or non-denominational group you're in. And although it is not recommended and the Bible admonishes us in Hebrews 10:25 not to forsake assembling together, a person can be a Christian even if he isn't a member of and/or doesn't meet with others in a church building. I was in this position for some time myself but would not recommend it. Being with other Christians strengthens us personally and gives us the opportunity to share our faith and fellowship with those who might need our encouragement even without us knowing it. I enjoy walking in the front doors of the church and fellowshipping with friends of like faith and sometimes sharing a meal with them.

I have been and will continue to talk about Jesus as Savior and Lord. As I say this, I realize there are a lot of people who believe there is a God or Supreme Being but do not believe that Jesus is the only way to spend eternity with God the Father who they may call Allah, the Man Upstairs, or some other name. They don't believe that faith in Jesus Christ is necessary for salvation, going to Heaven to be in the presence of God for eternity. I know there are a lot of influential folks, even REALLY GOOD, MORAL FOLKS who believe this way.

If this is your belief, I ask you to look at and pray about six quotes from the New Testament testifying about Jesus.

- First from Paul, possibly the greatest apostle and who wrote a lot of the New Testament: from Phillippians 3: 9-11 - *"And be found in him, not having mine own righteousness, which is of the law, but that which is through the faith of Christ, the righteousness which is of God by faith:* **That I may know him, and the power of his resurrection, and the fellowship of his sufferings, being made conformable unto his death; If by any means I might attain unto the resurrection of the dead.***"*

- Second from Peter, one of the three disciples closest to Jesus: from Acts 4: 10-12 - *"Be it known unto you all, and to all the people of Israel, that by the name of Jesus Christ of Nazareth, whom ye crucified, whom God raised from the dead, even by him doth this man stand here before you whole. This is the stone which was set at nought of you builders, which is become the head of the corner. Neither is there salvation in any other: for* **there is none other name under heaven given among men, whereby we must be saved.***"* This is God inspired scripture that, speaking of Christ, says by "none other name."

- Third from the Son of God Himself in John 14:6: *Jesus saith unto him, "I am the way, the truth, and the life:* **no man cometh unto the Father, but by me.***"*

God inspired scripture says *"no man cometh unto the Father but by Me"*, spoken by Jesus. I have read the New Testament from beginning to end as many of you have. Please bear with me and think about what the Holy Bible actually says. I believe you will see that what I am saying is scripturally true even though it may not be what many have been taught and want to hear. If we believe in the God of the Bible; if we believe that He is sovereign; if we believe that He alone can determine the road to Heaven, we have no right to decide for ourselves that there is any other way or even a variation of *the* Way. We do not have the authority to bypass God's design and purpose for humanity.

God the Father, Son, and Holy Spirit are the creators of the universe and everything in it. The Father spoke; Jesus created, and the Holy Spirit hovered over and breathed life into man. They were all three present and active at creation. Only the Godhead deserves our worship.

- Fourth - We need to read what the Father Himself said about Jesus. After Jesus was baptized and before he went into the wilderness to be tempted for 40 days, God said in Matthew 3:17 *"...This is my beloved Son, in whom I am well pleased."* This was at the beginning of Jesus's ministry.
- Fifth - And again when Jesus was transfigured before Peter, James, and John, when He spoke to Moses and Elias (Elijah), God Himself spoke from the cloud in Matthew 17:5 saying *"... This is my beloved Son, in whom I am well pleased; hear ye him."*

God would not have been well pleased with Jesus and allow Him to say that He, Jesus, is the only way to the Father if He were not. If Jesus were not the only way to salvation, God the Father would have been supporting a lie.

- Sixth - *Be it known unto you all, and to all the people of Israel, that by the name of Jesus Christ of Nazareth ... Neither is there salvation in any other:* **for there is none other name under heaven given among men, whereby we must be saved.** Acts 4:10-12 Nothing could be plainer.

I know some of you may disagree with what I have said. But either the Bible is true or it isn't. Either we listen to God or we ignore Him. If I believe that God is real and alive today and if I believe the Bible is the true, inspired word of God, I have to believe that Jesus is the only way to eternity with God the Father. Either the Bible is truly the inspired word of God, or it isn't. It can be only one way. Either Jesus lied in John 14:6, or He is the only way to the Father. And if He lied, can we believe anything else He said? What good is the Bible if part of it is false? We don't have the right to pick and choose what parts of the Bible we want to believe. We are walking on dangerous territory when we think or act like our beliefs are superior to the Word of God.

Sometimes what we have learned from those who came before us needs to be tested by the light of Scripture. **We alone are responsible for what we believe**, even if it's different than the beloved generations before us.

Along this same line, nowhere do I find in scripture that we are to pray to anyone other than the Godhead, not even Mary, the beloved mother of Jesus Himself. The apostles and close disciples of Jesus's day were spiritual men and women. They led many people to the Lord and today, 2,000 years later, they are responsible for the New Testament by which people hear the gospel and receive salvation. They were the ones chosen by Jesus Himself to begin the greatest spiritual revolution of all time through the leading of the Holy Spirit and Jesus's teachings.

But all the great women and men of the Bible are dead now and cannot do anything else for us. I cannot find anywhere that the Bible says we can seek guidance from any of them. The Godhead calls ministers of the gospel, whether laymen or clergy, to help mankind until they are no longer present here on this earth. When a human being dies, he can no longer be called on to assist the living, whether in conversation or prayer, no matter how spiritual he or she was. That is not the way God set it up. We cannot change this anymore than we can stop gravity. It's God's plan and that's the way it is.

Some may think that if we have received Christ as our Savior, there's no problem with speaking to the saints of old. That may sound reasonable at first glance, but it takes our attention away from Christ, our *one and only* mediator with God. Our focus needs to be on the only One who can come to our aid.

God said in Exodus 20:5, *"—for I the LORD thy God am a jealous God —."* He will not accept anyone else receiving praise or glory or even just being lifted higher than He has deemed their rightful place.

The important thing here is that God was and is speaking to His people, those living then, now, and in the future. His word is living. It is still alive in the 21st century and always will be.

When He gave us 2 Chronicles 7:14, He was literally speaking to the Jews, descendants of Abraham. Today, as explained in Romans 2:28, 29 and Mark 16:15 above, either a Jew or a Gentile can be one of His people if they receive Jesus as Savior. These are the ones who can pray and seek God's face in humility and turn the tide for America. Hopefully, you either are or will become one of His people and help turn our country back to God by fulfilling His direction as a way of life. This is a lifestyle that allows God to have his proper place in your life which is much more than specific acts or just living a good moral life.

Salvation Is for "Whosever"

I need to diverge before the next chapter and present the scriptures that were given in the New Testament that lead to salvation. Only by salvation can we be called His people. Please don't skip the next few paragraphs, even if you think they don't apply to you. You may be able to use them for someone you love.

There may be some readers who have not placed their trust in Jesus. Maybe you yourself are a moral, respected person in your community; you have been baptized and maybe even teach Sunday

School; you go to church and serve the church; you give to the poor and you treat everyone with the respect they deserve. But the pressing question is "Have you given yourself to Jesus, or just to the church?

If you have not received Christ as the only way to the Father; if you have not asked Him to be your Savior and Lord, I encourage you to meditate on the following verses. They are the inspired word of Creator and Father God who loves you and desires more than anything else in the world for you to enter His Kingdom and spend eternity with Him.

Romans 3:23 - *For all have sinned, and come short of the glory of God;* That's every one of us: me, you, your neighbor, your loved ones, everyone.

Romans 6:23 - *For the wages of sin is death; but the gift of God is eternal life through Jesus Christ our Lord.* Spiritual death should not be your eternity. True life is for you. It is the greatest gift you will ever receive. But you must receive it. It's yours for the asking, no strings attached, with the promise of an abundant life forevermore if you will just receive it.

Romans 5:8 - *But God commendeth his love toward us, in that, while we were yet sinners, Christ died for us.* We are the sinners, not Christ. It is our debt, but He paid it in full on the cross. A terrible death for him; a glorious, eternal life for you.

Romans 10:9, 10 - *That if thou shalt confess with thy mouth the Lord Jesus, and shalt believe in thine heart that God hath raised him from the dead, thou shalt be saved. For with the heart man believeth unto righteousness; and with the mouth confession is made unto salvation.* How much easier could it be? Confess, believe, and you will receive. You might wonder if it could really be that easy. But it is. God wouldn't trick or lie to you. He gives you the offer of eternal salvation and an abundant life. But He won't force it on you. Take it! It's your choice.

Ephesians 2:8, 9 - *For by grace are ye saved through faith; and that not of yourselves: it is the gift of God: Not of works, lest any man should boast.* Please don't wait until you are worthy of salvation. It will never happen. God gives you the understanding of how to receive salvation and the faith to do so. Grace has been explained as <u>G</u>od's <u>r</u>iches <u>at</u> <u>C</u>hrist's <u>e</u>xpense. The debt has been paid. Receive eternal salvation now.

Matthew 10:32, 33 - *Whosoever therefore shall confess me* (Jesus) *before men, him will I confess also before my Father which is in heaven. But whosoever shall deny me before men, him will I also deny before my Father which is in heaven.* Jesus is the only way to salvation. He will be mediator between you and the Father. He died for you. Let Him confess you to His Father so you can also call Him Father.

John 3:16 - *For God so loved the world, that he gave his only begotten Son, that whosoever believeth in him should not perish, but have everlasting life.* You are a "whosoever" if you will only believe *in* Jesus. This is more than just believing Christ once lived as a human being, died a physical death, and rose to Heaven. Believing *in* Christ is totally different than believing *about* Him.

You might also want to look at the Addendum in the back of this book.

We need to understand that salvation is based on our own individual relationship with Christ. It is good that parents dedicate their children as infants or during early childhood. But that child must give himself or herself to Jesus later on. We cannot enter heaven on our parent's faith or their actions on our behalf. The decision must be made personally.

The scriptures above talk about faith, the heart, believing, and confessing in order to receive the gift of salvation through faith in Christ.

But too often, a person will become convicted of their sin and in emotional desperation make a "profession of faith" that is not from the heart, but from fear or guilt, but there is no change in his or her life afterward. John the Baptist said in Matthew 3:2, *"...Repent ye: for the kingdom of heaven is at hand."*

From the Savior Himself, we read in Matthew 4:17, *"From that time Jesus began to preach, and to say, Repent: for the kingdom of heaven is at hand."* Repentance is more than asking for forgiveness. Repentance is making a change in lifestyle and belief. It's turning form the life we were leading to a life submitted to God through our Lord Jesus as led by the Holy Spirit.

CHAPTER 4

Shall Humble Themselves

★ ★ ★ ★

When God says we must humble ourselves, He is not saying we are unimportant. Our thoughts about the words "humble" and "humility" are often negative or we think of them in terms of personal weakness. But God views humility in His people as a very good thing, quite different than what we sometimes think. We are made in His image and we are the favorite of all His creation. I have heard it said speaking of mankind, "God didn't make no junk!"

When we humble ourselves in the sight of God, we are putting Him above everything and everyone else. We are saying everything about us - our very being - is subject to Him, honors Him, and glorifies Him. Rather than making me less of a person, humility before God elevates me. Someone said, "Humility is not thinking less of yourself, but thinking of yourself less." We might also say that humility is not thinking less of ourselves, but simply thinking more of Him and even of others.

Humble yourselves in the sight of the Lord, and he shall lift you up. James 4:10

Whosoever therefore shall humble himself as this little child, the same is greatest in the kingdom of heaven. Matthew 18:4

Humble yourselves therefore under the mighty hand of God, that he may exalt you in due time: 1 Peter 5:6

In each of these verses God instructs us to humble ourselves. He wants us to make the decision to do so. Although He can create or allow situations that humiliate us and bring us to our knees, that is not the way He wants us to become humble. In each scripture above He lifts us up only after we humble ourselves. If (there's that word again) we take the initiative, the reward is great. I'm working at this, but have not achieved the level of humility I need or even desire. Maybe you're right there with me.

Humility is the first step given by God, a vital key I believe, to activating the promise in 2 Chronicles 7:14. Without it the healing of our nation will not occur. If you have always thought prayer is *the* key, that prayer is all we need, please bear with me. Prayer is a crucial, absolutely vital part of our nation's healing. But it's not the whole thing. We Christians have within our grasp the four keys to unlock a glorious future for our children and grandchildren. Who would refuse to do that for their young'uns? So what is involved in humility, the first key God lists?

Let nothing be done through strife or vainglory; but in lowliness of mind let each esteem other better than themselves. Phil 2:3

In our society; in business, politics, sports, and often even in churches the objective of many, if not most of us, is to please ourselves or to be number one. We may not say it, but we often think of ourselves as number one. Our needs and our desires come before anything or anyone else. I understand that; it's the way we humans naturally think. But that's not God-think. His thoughts are above our thoughts. They don't make sense to the human mind. It's like the thoughts of a parent to a two year old who wants his way all the time.

When a lawyer asked Jesus in Matthew 22 which was the greatest commandment, Jesus replied in vv. 37-40, "*...Thou shalt love the Lord* *thy God with all thy heart, and with all thy soul, and with all thy mind. This is the first and great commandment. And the second is like unto it, Thou shalt love thy neighbour as thyself. On these two commandments hang all the law and the prophets."*

Whether we act like it or not, most of us know in our minds that the greatest commandment is to love God. But if given the opportunity to categorize the commandments in order of importance how many of us would put loving others second? I know as well as you do that it is extremely difficult to love some people. So if God said it's so important, how do we love these folks?

This is a much deeper study than we can go into here and even if we could, I'm not qualified to teach it. But we can't ignore it because: "*Therefore to him that knoweth to do good, and doeth it not, to him it is sin.*" James 4:17. No matter how much we'd like to, we can't make this scripture go away.

I'm not a psychiatrist, but I think if we truly want to do God's will in this matter we can begin by acting and speaking as if we have God's love for others. I'm not talking about faking it. I'm talking about taking first steps to fulfilling the second greatest commandment. As we begin acting a certain way and keep it up, maybe even developing a habit, we grow in that area.

I can look at that person that really irritates me and remind myself, "God loves him and Christ died for him just as He died for me. So I need to treat him as if Christ were standing beside him, seeing my every action, hearing my every word, and reading my every thought." After all, He is.

When that guy cuts me off on the highway, I need to remember that I might have the opportunity to witness to him some day. If that opportunity comes, how can I tell him about the love of God if he remembers that I laid on the horn, shook my fist at him, and screamed at the top of my lungs? After all, I've done some dumb and dangerous things behind the wheel myself.

The apostle Paul said in I Timothy 5:20 (KJV), *"Them that sin rebuke before all, that others also may fear."* Other translations make this a little clearer. He's talking about rebuking those who continue in sin on a regular basis, not just making a mistake which is out of character. But that doesn't give us an excuse to gossip or talk about someone behind their back. That was a regular occurrence in the early church and since man's inner thoughts haven't changed it's prevalent in the body of Christ even today. Gossiping and backbiting have no place in the body of Christ. If tempted to do so I must remember that I'm talking about one of God's children and the Father doesn't like it.

When I see others in need it is not my place to judge them. There are those that society looks down on. Maybe they actually could do better or maybe they don't know where to begin, even if they want to. God hasn't given me the right to judge them even if they are doing less than what they can. So what if they do waste the few dollars I give them? It's not going to put me in bankruptcy and it just might give them a little encouragement as well as letting them get a burger. The point is they are loved by God, no matter their race, ethnicity, social standing, financial situation, occupation, or any other standard mankind has chosen to establish. Since God loves them, I am wrong in judging. Maybe I'm even sinning. It's been said, "If you can't say something nice, don't say anything." We as Christians can take a step forward and do more for others.

Andrew Murray wrote a book simply entitled "Humility" which I would highly recommend to anyone who wants a deeper study on this powerful attribute which God loves in His people.

Pride:

And then there's pride, that terrible attitude that hurts those we're in contact with and eventually ourselves.

There are obviously different levels and objects of pride. It is human nature to take pride in some things and people. I am proud of each member of my family. I don't think there's anything wrong with that as long as I don't let my feelings for them interfere with my relationship to God or cause pride to make them think they are better than anyone else. I am proud of my country, but I can't put country above God. As the song goes, I am proud to be an American. But I must remember that I had nothing to do with making this nation great and I had nothing to do with when or where I was born or to whom I was born. I am just the recipient of many tremendous blessings.

Taking pride in others (if that's the correct word) is different than being proud of ourselves, who we are or what we've done.

We read in Proverbs 6:16-19, "*These six things* doth the *Lord hate: yea, seven are an **abomination** unto him: A proud look, a lying tongue, and hands that shed innocent blood, An heart that deviseth wicked imaginations, feet that be swift in running to mischief, A false witness that speaketh lies, and he that soweth discord among brethren.*" I emboldened two words in verse 16: "hate" and "abomination". These are extremely harsh words telling how God feels about seven specific things. The first thing listed is pride.

As a good person, I bet you don't like a habitual liar, a person who sheds innocent blood, a person who devises wickedness or mischief, or a person who is a false witness or stirs up trouble. Yet God lumps a proud person with these. In fact, He calls them all an abomination. Pride is an abomination to God! Many of us, myself included, need to sit back and really think about this. Pride is a dangerous, terrible force, even in the church today.

A "proud look" is synonymous with arrogance, being boastful, or thinking more highly of one's self than others (same as looking down on others). Our pride can, and often does, even cause us to put ourselves and our thoughts above God's purpose in our lives. I know it's not intentional, but it's a fact. The proof is in the messes we get ourselves into that wouldn't have happened if we had been pursuing God's will for our lives rather than our own ambitions.

I heard a teaching by Joyce Meyer in which she rightly stated that pride is the cause of many kinds of sins including indifference to other people's needs, anger, bitterness, bad tempers, and un-forgiveness. The list could go on and on.

Pride caused the very first sin when Satan thought himself to be equal with God. Pride was also the cause of the first murder when Cain killed his brother Abel. Thinking about all these things, no wonder God hates it so much.

As human beings it is normal (not right, but normal) for us to take pride in our work and our accomplishments. But we must remember how we got our ability to perform. *Every good gift and every perfect gift is from above, and cometh down from the Father of lights, with whom is no variableness, neither shadow of turning.* James 1:17 If we boast in anything, it should be in the Lord.

The athlete should remember that he did not create his body. He did have to exercise it in order to excel in his sport, but he had nothing to do with his being born with certain talents. He has no right to think of himself as being better than someone else, even, or maybe especially, if he is one of those who has become wealthy because of his abilities.

The wealthy CEO of a successful company has certainly contributed to that success because of his talents, knowledge, tenacity, and devotion to his job. But he didn't create the brain that allows him to imagine, foresee, and do things that others cannot do.

Great musicians and artists were born with abilities that most of us don't have and therefore cannot develop to the extent of a top performer. They should use these talents to inspire and bless others, not to gloat. When we are blessed we should bless others.

But what about us ordinary folks that don't stand out above the crowd? It may not be so obvious, but we too are subject to pride in ourselves. If I achieve something or someone gives me a compliment, my head begins to swell and I have to remind myself that I could do nothing if I had not been born with the ability to do it. I did not always understand this and it has become my "thorn in the flesh". In my writing, I make it a point to give God the glory if someone tells me what I wrote is good. But even then, a little pride tends to sneak in and I have to quickly ask God to forgive me. And I can just have a pretty good thought about something or an inspiration and I have a tendency to be proud of my intellect. But then again I have to ask for forgiveness. I would hate to know how many times I have had to ask for forgiveness due to my pride. Unfortunately, I imagine God will tell me some day.

A man's pride shall bring him low: Proverbs 29:23a. I have experienced that greatly.

God resisteth the proud, James 4:6a Unfortunately, we may not even realize it if things are going good for us in the world.

From these scriptures, especially the last, it appears that pride in who we are can hinder our prayers. If God resists the proud, it seems to me that He would hold such a one at arm's length; not that He doesn't love him and won't forgive him. But our Heavenly Father knows he would find little or no spiritual satisfaction until he submits to God. Could it be that He wouldn't respond to many prayers of the excessively proud except one of repentance of that pride and a sincere pleading to be forgiven by God?

Paul said in Romans 12:3, "*For I say, through the grace given unto me, to every man that is among you, not to think of himself more highly than he ought to think; but to think soberly, according as God hath dealt to every man the measure of faith.*" When we approach God in prayer we must recognize that only He is worthy of praise.

Praise given to us by others can cause us to lift ourselves up in our own eyes (pride), thus limiting our ability to commune with the Source of everything good. Pride builds a barrier to an intimate relationship with the Father and hinders the effectiveness of our prayers. James 5:16 says, "*The effectual, fervent prayer of a righteous man availeth much.*" It doesn't say the prayer of a proud man availeth much.

Righteousness

A simple explanation of righteousness is to be in right standing with God. The scriptures above show a proud man is not in right standing with God. This is not to say pride keeps us from being saved, but it does hinder our relationship with the Father. Most of us have some level of pride, some more than others. I believe without a doubt as pride increases righteousness automatically decreases. Fortunately the opposite is true. As we allow God to burn that pride out of us, our righteousness increases. As I say this, I realize that it could create some confusion because scripture says that we are the righteousness of God.

For he hath made him to be sin for us, who knew no sin; that we might be made the righteousness of God in him. 2 Corinthians 5:21. Righteousness is a deep study that we can't get into here, and again, I'm not qualified to teach it even if we had the space. In my limited understanding, there are at least two aspects of righteousness. Suffice it here to say that one aspect is *positional* and the other is *relational*. 2 Corinthians 5:21 is speaking of our position in the body of Christ. When He died on the cross, taking the punishment of our sins upon

Himself, He made us sinless in the eyes of God as pertains to our eternity. We who receive Christ and His atoning death will spend eternity in Heaven. Since Jesus took our sins on himself, we are positionally righteous in God's eyes.

But the relational side of righteousness pertains to my daily relationship with the Father. No-one would consider me as relationally righteous as the Apostle Paul in my daily life. This aspect of righteousness pertains to walking in the Spirit, seeking daily to grow in my love for God and faith in Him. We are made righteous positionally when we receive Christ as Savior. Every Christian is right there with the apostle positionally. And we grow in righteousness relationally as we draw nearer to God. As we do so, humility increases.

America: Humble or Too Proud for Our Own Good?

We in America have much to be grateful for. Unfortunately, we have a tendency to pat ourselves on the back and claim credit for those things that have been provided by others, and all because of the grace of God. A self-made man is the object of praise. We praise our athletes and movie stars. And as we praise them, we are only feeding their self-esteem, contributing to their pride in themselves. In effect, we are doing them a disfavor spiritually.

As adults, it is our responsibility to encourage our children. Unfortunately, we often praise them until they become proud of themselves, not understanding that when they excel in any area, whether it be sports, academics, or any other endeavor, it is because they are utilizing a gift the origin of which they had nothing to do. That was my story in my youth and for too many years in adulthood. If we do not train our children with the understanding that what they have is a gift, we are contributing to the pride God detests. This is a terrible thing to do to our children.

It is important for us to realize when our pride holds us back individually. And the combined individual pride of God's people can hold our nation back. Proverbs 16:18 says, "*Pride goeth before destruction, and an haughty spirit before a fall.*" I pray that we as a nation of proud individuals will humble ourselves and begin to give God His rightful honor rather than see our nation fall.

Ezekiel 16:49 says, "*Behold, this was the iniquity of thy sister Sodom, **pride, fulness of bread, and abundance of idleness** was in her and in her daughters, **neither did she strengthen the hand of the poor and needy**.*" We know what happened to Sodom. Reading back over this scripture, can the same iniquity be said about America today? If we really contemplate those emboldened words and phrases above I think we will see modern America.

Has our abundance contributed to a "me, me, me" attitude? Yes, we are a giving people, especially in times of trouble, but often for many of us, our individual giving usually comes after our own desires (not necessarily needs) are met. We (myself included) are often self-indulgent to the extent that others don't receive the blessings God intended us to give them. This kind of giving of ourselves and our possessions is not socialism because it is voluntary, not mandated by government; it is joyfully fulfilling God's plan for mankind.

Hosea 5:5 speaks of God's chosen people: *And the pride of Israel doth testify to his face: therefore shall Israel and Ephraim fall in their iniquity; Judah also shall fall with them*. If God allowed His chosen people to fall because of pride why would He not allow that for any other nation, including the USA?

The Bible speaks of pride of the heart. Pride of the heart causes us to place our priorities in things other than God. Family, work, hobbies, other interests, and play are all vital parts of human life. God Himself has provided in His great plan for all these things to contribute to a healthy, well-rounded life. But they have to be in their proper place.

When we allow them to come before God and our relationship with Him, this reveals pride of heart replacing God in our lives. We do not physically bow down to them and do not worship them in religious terms, but these things actually become idols to us.

Personalizing 2 Chronicles 7:14

In the subtitle of this book, "God's Answer for America's Troubles", I am stating that America has a problem and He has the answer. That answer is you and me doing what He has prescribed as the cure for a fateful disease. He has given us a challenge. If we take the challenge and carry it to the finish line, we will have activated the cure for our great nation's dilemma.

The cure comes in four doses:

> Humility before God,
>
> Prayer,
>
> Seeking His face, *and*
>
> Turning from our wicked ways (repenting).

The word "or" is nowhere to be found in 2 Chronicles 7:14. We have to take all the doses for a cure. None of them are easy. It doesn't happen overnight. It's a process that takes time and it is not a piece of cake. But there is icing on the cake at the finish line when it's over. We'll not win the prize if we fall short and quit before the time is completed.

Humility is one dose we'd like to ignore but we can't. Though extremely important, a simple prayer alone won't cut it. I believe humility is a prerequisite for a deep prayer life, one that touches God and causes Him to do what He said He'll do, what He *wants* to do **IF....**

I am speaking here of changed lives; lives that allow the God of the universe to be our own personal God, the God that replaces "things" in our daily lives; the God that will make good lives even better when they are submitted to Him in humility; the God that will save this nation when His people come to Him in humility, recognizing God as our all in all and we are nothing without Him.

The road is rough but the reward is worth it. The 23rd Psalm might help us understand humility a little better. I would guess every reader has heard it and many have memorized it in one translation or another, especially if we grew up in church. What could be more humble than a lamb depending on its master for everything: food, water, protection, and guidance?

The first three verses speak *about* God. In the last three David is talking to God. I like to say all six verses as if I were speaking *to* Him. Instead of saying "He" I like to say "You". It helps me draw near to my Creator if I'm consciously speaking directly to Him. I then put a little twist at the very end as follows.

__You__, LORD, __are__ my shepherd; I shall not want.

__You__ maketh me to lie down in green pastures: __you__ leadeth me beside the still waters.

__You__ restoreth my soul: __you__ leadeth me in the paths of righteousness for __your__ name's sake.

Yea, though I walk through the valley of the shadow of death, I will fear no evil: for thou art with me; thy rod and thy staff they comfort me

Thou preparest a table before me in the presence of mine enemies: thou anointest my head with oil; my cup runneth over.

Surely goodness and mercy shall follow me all the days of my life: and I will __be a__ house of the LORD for ever.

I said "a" house rather than "the" house because I'm one of many. As New Testament children of God, we are His temple. He no longer dwells in a tent or temple made with human hands. He dwells in His people. *Know ye not that ye are the temple of God, and that the Spirit of God dwelleth in you?* 1 Corinthians 3:16 I can therefore say "I will be a house of the Lord forever."

God created man in His own image. He now dwells in us as the Holy Spirit. In spite of all our faults, weaknesses, and inabilities we are His dwelling place; the dwelling place of the great I Am. We are one with the Father, Son, and Holy Ghost.

As we meditate on this we can realize that the Greatest Being in all the universe and beyond indwells us and wants to provide all our needs. We can then begin to humble ourselves before Him because of our great needs and inability to fulfill those needs without His strength in us. We are the lambs dependent on the great Shepherd, our own personal Shepherd.

CHAPTER 5

And Pray

★ ★ ★ ★

The most simple and yet accurate definition of prayer is "speaking with God". Of all the life forms He put on this earth, we are the only one with the ability to commune with the Creator of the universe. This is how I usually think about prayer. But when contemplating this chapter the following thought came to me. Prayer is when a fallible, immature, weak, undeserving, very limited human being is allowed to be in the presence of and speak to the perfect, faultless, all powerful, everlasting Creator of the universe, God Himself. Few of us will be allowed to enter the White House to speak to POTUS, especially without an appointment. But we can enter the presence of the Almighty at any time, 24/7. We don't have to go to Gabriel or Peter for an appointment. How awesome is that?

We often take prayer for granted. We may have a short prayer when we get up in the morning, or when we go to bed if we remember, feel like it, and have time. We ask God's blessings on our meals, maybe in the same words each time and often without thought of what we're saying or to Whom we're speaking.

Since it's only the two of us at home now, my wife and I usually sit in the family room to eat after she asks the blessing while we're in the kitchen getting our meals together. More than once I've had to ask her after I sat down if we've asked the blessing. Apparently to me it was just a formality. Now I purposely set my mind on the Lord as we pray.

Prayer, whether brief or long and at any occasion, should be a sacred event. We are being given the opportunity, a gift in itself, to address Almighty God. We should think of prayer as an opportunity, not a habit or a prerequisite for something.

Let's assume for just a moment that it would be possible for every Christian in this country to set aside an hour to pray on a specific day at a given time so we would all be praying to our heavenly Father at the same time. And we would be basing this act on 2 Chronicles 7:14. What do you think would happen?

In the first place, I doubt if most of us could actually pray for an hour. We would all begin at the same time and a select few would still be praying at the end of the hour. What about the rest of us? What happened within that hour? In a few minutes, maybe seconds, my mind went off on a tangent. Some of you probably went there with me. I got back on track for a brief time and then I found myself thinking about what I need to do this afternoon. Back on track again. Then, I wonder if I took the fish out of the freezer for supper. And on it would go until I realized that only 13 minutes had passed and I didn't know what else to pray about. Should I just repeat what little I'd already said?

Let's make another assumption. Let's pretend all of us, even me, did pray for an hour. Then we went back to what we were doing. The next day we did what we always do on that day and for the rest of the week; the month; the year.

All of His people in the nation had joined together for an hour and prayed because He told us He would save our nation "IF—". In the near future, would we begin to see our country as a whole turning back to

God because of our faithfulness to pray for our country's healing for an hour? I seriously doubt it.

We have a day set aside for prayer for the nation. That is certainly longer than the hour I spoke of. But in reality, I think the same thing would apply to the day as to the hour. I applaud and support those who do this regularly and am not knocking the day of prayer. I'm all for any prayer, whether short or long. I'm just trying to make a point. The salvation of this nation could begin with a day of prayer, but it is ultimately dependent on a lifelong way of living by a whole bunch of God's people. If I've offended anyone, I ask you to look at the heart and depth of the matter.

In the first place prayer, though vital, is only ¼ of the formula for healing. There's also humility, seeking His face, and turning from our wickedness. All four elements of this instruction are necessary. God doesn't waste His breath, so He wouldn't have spoken those words if they weren't important. If a day of prayer were all it would take, He would have said so. And we would not be in the spiritual trough we're in now. We have had a day of prayer for a long time and yet our nation is getting farther and farther away from God each passing year. We must be missing something.

Secondly, in chapter two, I made the statement "—in verse 14 God is talking not just about a quick prayer, brief activity, sacrifice, or ceremony to undertake to save the Israelite nation, but about a **personal relationship** with His people—". At the end of chapter four I mentioned **changed lives**. The four parts of the "if" show He wants dedication from His people for much longer than an hour or a day in only one aspect of our lives.

God wants more than what many of us are willing to give Him. He wants lives that are totally committed to Him. He wants more than quick prayers when we remember or when there's an immediate need. He wants more than meeting with Him twice on Sunday and maybe

Wednesday evening. He wants more than a regular day at the soup kitchen or food pantry. He wants more than giving a stranger's child or an orphan a gift on Christmas. He does want all that. But there's something more important to Him. He wants **US** as we do all these things. He wants our very being. When I yield to His Lordship, these works will follow, but they do not precede or replace a personal relationship.

Praise and worship

I grew up in a church with a bunch of really fine Christians. The older ones are gone now, but I still think about some of them and thank God for what they meant to me. We were taught to read the Bible and pray individually, taking our needs and those of others to the Lord in prayer. We sang the hymns of worship corporately. But I don't recall being taught to have a time of personal praise and worship, just me and my Father. Maybe I just forgot. But I wonder how many of us regularly set apart a time to worship, praise, and voice our love to Him, whether audibly or quietly.

Psalm 100:4 tells us how we should approach God in prayer, "*Enter into his gates with thanksgiving, and into his courts with praise: be thankful unto him, and bless his name.*" This should come before petitions and repentance. It isn't that God needs it. It's more that we need to take time to recognize the awesomeness of the One Who we're going to be addressing.

What is it about thanksgiving? 1 Thessalonians 5:18 reads, "*In every thing give thanks: for this is the will of God in Christ Jesus concerning you.*" Some interpret this as saying we are to be grateful for everything that comes our way but I don't think this is accurate. The scripture says, "*In* everything...". It doesn't say, "for" everything. I believe this means that *in* every situation, good or bad, we need to be thanking God for His goodness, Who He is, and what He will work out for us in each situation if we give it to Him.

In Romans 8:28, the apostle Paul said, "*And we know that all things work together for good to them that love God, to them who are the called according to his purpose.*" As we praise and worship God in all circumstances He will encourage us and either show us the way or work it out Himself. But we must trust Him enough to surrender whatever it is to Him.

This scripture doesn't say everything that happens is good. It says God will work everything for good if we allow Him to do it. It may not be what we wanted, but it will work out for His glory.

Pray without ceasing

He wants me to desire Him so much that I praise Him and pray throughout the day whether playing, relaxing, or working. When I'm in the car I could spend some time praising God rather than listening to the radio or a tape from the time I turn the ignition key until I reach my destination. There's nothing wrong with listening to music if it's moral, especially if it's spiritual. But He would appreciate us spending at least part of that ride praising and thanking Him.

If you live out in the country like I do, you can praise Him for the beautiful creation of nature all around as you drive down the road or just step out into your back yard. And if you don't live in the country I'm sure there is something for which you can give thanks and praise to God. Just look around at His creation and consider the things you have which people in third world countries, and even tens of thousands right here in America, don't have. Even if you have no possessions or a place to lay your head, you can be thankful you are free to worship as you please if you desire to do so.

Some of us listen to good music while we're mowing the lawn. But it's so much better to sing praises to the Lord as we're circling the house on or behind a noisy mower. I do so even with a less than pleasant voice since no-one can hear me. And even on a bad day at work or school we have so much we can pray about. We all have friends and family members who need to be lifted up in prayer. And recreation or vacation really gives us something to be thankful for.

We could go on and on about how we could praise him during the day. We can begin by counting our many blessings and we can thank God for each one as they come our way or as they come to mind, not waiting until we go to bed. We can make lists of people who need prayer and pray for the homeless guy when we see him on the sidewalk. We don't know his situation and a prayer for him would be much more beneficial than judgement which will help no-one. We could daily pray for our coworkers and the company we work for. We could minister to that hurting one at the water cooler. We can ask the Lord to help us be open to opportunities to help people and be witnesses for Him throughout the day through the Holy Spirit Who indwells every Christian.

I'm not suggesting praying at these times could replace consistently, diligently setting aside time for quiet prayer and meditation on the Lord and His Word. These prayers are in addition to my special closet prayer. They are extra time to spend with the Master of our day and help us draw nearer to Him.

My point is God wants to be the center of our attention. I'm not so naive as to believe we won't think of other things as we go about our daily tasks. I certainly do and God knows we have to pay attention to what we're doing. We have to make a living to support our families; we have to nourish and pay attention to our kids; and we need some entertainment to break up a stressful week. All this is necessary for a balanced life, but He wants more than an occasional prayer shot His way. He would really be pleased if my thoughts were directed to Him in thanksgiving and praise as well as petitions when I need something as I go about my day, all day.

I truly believe as my prayer life increases, those stresses of work and life in general will decrease. That would be peace, one of the fruits of the Spirit. The fruits of the Spirit develop only as our relationship with God grows. That relationship grows only as we commune with Him and become more aware of Him in our daily walk, 24/7.

1 Thessalonians 5:17 says, "*Pray without ceasing*". There was a French monk named Brother Lawrence in the 17th century who made on-going prayer a regular part of his day. When called to a specific time of prayer by his superior, he obediently went, but said this specified time for prayer was no different than his working day because he was constantly speaking to His Father. Few of us will ever have such a level of prayer, but it gives me a fresh understanding of what a day intentionally and consciously spent in the presence of Jesus could be like.

And of course we should pray for our country and leaders at all levels on a daily basis. That's what we generally think about when we read 2 Chronicles 7:14. The Bible instructs us to pray for those who are over us, not only on spiritual levels, but also in the government. This is important to our Father.

But surprisingly, this particular scripture says nothing about praying for the country or its leaders. Rather He speaks of individual humility, prayer, seeking His face, and turning from our wicked ways. He is speaking of a personal relationship. Just as works automatically follow a relationship with God on our part, forgiveness and healing follow a relationship on God's part. He wants each of us to have a lifestyle centered on Him. He has no interest in being left in the closet or shut behind church doors when we leave the building.

Although I've said all this to you, I must admit, although I pray regularly, I am not a prayer warrior as are some folks I know, maybe you. There is always room for improvement but change is difficult. Growing pains are relevant to spiritual growth as much as they are to physical growth, maybe more so because spiritual growth when truly sought after lasts a lifetime, not just 18 or 20 years. But growth leads to maturity and maturity doesn't come overnight. Neither does a strong prayer life. We cannot and should not expect to become prayer warriors just because we would like to. We need to remember, God looks at the heart and appreciates any effort we make. But we should not use that as an excuse not to be more diligent in our prayer life

The old saying, "Practice makes perfect" applies to prayer life as much as to any other endeavor. Although it may be difficult to work out the time or develop the discipline, we need to remember any journey begins with the first step and we do not reach the destination without many steps. We don't have the opportunity to be "beamed up" to spiritual maturity or a powerful prayer life.

I think one reason it's difficult to develop a life of prayer is because we don't physically see to Whom we're talking and very seldom if ever will most of us audibly hear Him speak. If I could physically see the Father, Jesus, or the Holy Spirit I think it would be easier to carry on a conversation with Them, but that hasn't happened. This is where faith comes in. I find it personally helpful to mentally assert or maybe even envision speaking to the one and only God who is alive and wants to commune with me. I sometimes begin by looking at one of Diane's paintings of a nature scene hanging on my bedroom wall. I thank God for the beauty of His creation in the mountains, the lake, and the ducks flying over the lake as I begin my prayer with thanksgiving and praise.

That kind of mental imagery might not appeal to you, but if you have difficulty praying, I would encourage you to ask God to help you find a way to commit your thoughts to Him. It isn't always easy, but it will certainly have its rewards.

Dick Eastman wrote a very good book entitled, "No Easy Road: Discover the Extraordinary Power of Personal Prayer". He says prayer is the most remarkable act a human can perform and though sometimes difficult, it unleashes God's power. I've read this book more than once and keep it handy to read again.

He also wrote "The Hour That Changes the World: A Practical Plan for Personal Prayer." Although you may not be able to envision an hour in prayer, it gives practical suggestions about how readers can revitalize their prayer lives and develop a more consistent habit of daily prayer. You might even get to the point where an hour isn't enough time for you to commune with the Father as much as you'd like. Wouldn't that be awesome?

Before I leave this chapter, encouraging everyone to pray more, there are a couple of statements I need to make.

First, talking about praying without ceasing and praying for an hour can be daunting. I believe in everything I have said about prayer. But we can let the effort become a burden and legalistic. I believe God would rather I pray for ten or twenty minutes in complete subjection to His power and purpose in my life while leaning back in my recliner than to dutifully spend an hour on my knees; glancing at the clock; hoping the minute hand would move faster; and trying to figure out what to say to fill the next forty five minutes. He wants my heart more than my time.

But I also believe as our personal relationship with God grows, the ten minutes will turn into twenty, then maybe even an hour or more. Please understand, I'm not trying to justify a short prayer when God's desire for us is to learn to talk to Him often and in length as we would to a good friend. I'm just saying we need to begin where we are, but not limit ourselves in what we can practically learn to do. I have read of one great prayer warrior who said the more he had to do in a day, the longer he prayed before his day started. Lord, let that be me, or rather, Holy Spirit help me to become like him.

The second thing I need to say is a consistent, focused prayer life for many of us, maybe most, is not an easy thing to accomplish. We can sincerely determine we are going to pray on a regular basis and/ or to pray more often. Then for various reasons, depending on the individual and circumstances, we often do not succeed. Then we find ourselves in a state of self-condemnation and we give up because we just don't have it in us. But I think sometimes when we make the decision to pray more, we have often tried do it on our own, sort of like a New Year's Eve resolution that seldom succeeds. We fail to realize we need to ask God to help us. The more I grow in the Lord, the more I realize how weak I am when it comes to submitting specific things and ultimately my very being to Him. I have to pray for faith and strength constantly.

Paul tells us in Philippians 2:13 "*For it is God which worketh in you both to will and to do of his good pleasure.*" It is in His good pleasure when we want to improve our spiritual lives. According to this scripture, He works the desire (will) in us; it isn't that all of a sudden we came up with it on our own. As Christians, the Holy Spirit is constantly working in us to help us become what the Father desires us to be. When we are living in the Spirit He works His desires in us and they become our desires. Like salvation, it is grace which allows us to become sanctified.

Determining to pray more

So now He has given us the desire to improve our prayer life. What do we do next? We set up a plan and struggle to make it happen with our own self-determination. Going back to Philippians 2:13 we realize we have left Him out of the second part, *to do*. What we should have done was to say something like, "Father, You have given me the desire to commune with You in a deeper way. I thank You and praise You for doing that. Now I ask You to work it out in me as Your Word says You want to do. Give me the faith that You will help me pray when I don't feel like it or haven't seen the results I was expecting."

We may still develop a plan, but now we realize that we develop the plan with His leading and we accomplish the plan in His strength, not our own. How many times have we tried to walk closer to the Lord and failed? It was probably because we were trying to accomplish a good thing in our own strength. The "thing" was good, but the "working" was not. We need to remember: God is patient when His children are trying, just as a parent is patient with his baby when the baby is trying to learn to talk or walk.

Psalm 37:23 tells us *"The steps of a good man are ordered by the LORD: and he delighteth in his way."* Yes, we take the steps whether they be physical, mental, or spiritual. But He is the One Who has "ordered" or directed us to do so through His Holy Spirit Who indwells us. It really wasn't our bright, super-spiritual idea at all to begin praying more. We were open to Him and He gave us the desire for it, His desire for us. As we are open to the Spirit of God, His thoughts and desires become ours.

As Paul said in 1 Corinthians 3:16, *"Know ye not that ye are the temple of God, and that the Spirit of God dwelleth in you?"* Jesus Himself, speaking of the Holy Spirit, said in John 14:17 *"...for he dwelleth with you, and shall be in you."* The Holy Spirit is the Spirit of God Himself. Since He dwells in us, we have the power of God the Almighty Creator available to become what He desires us to be. Until we understand the power for successful living within us and really get it into our thought process, we will struggle in our own weakness, not taking advantage of the strength of God Himself abiding in us.

In the last few years I have come to realize just how weak I am in spiritual matters. But He is strong in me. He tells me I should pray and He will strengthen me to do His will by the power of the Holy Spirit Who dwells in me 24/7. The Holy Spirit doesn't take long vacations or even short breaks. He is always at work in us. If we can really understand that God loves us beyond measure; Jesus gave His life for us, and the Holy Spirit indwells us and is constantly working in us for our benefit, we can be overcomers of any obstacle hindering a closer walk with our heavenly Father.

Think about this. There is a vast universe out there filled with thousands of stars, comets, planets and I don't know what all. If someone were on the moon looking down at the state you live in, what would he see? I guarantee he wouldn't see you, a minute human being. And yet the God of the universe, that great expanse and everything we see and even things we can't imagine, sees you clearly. We are mere, weak mortals in this great universe, but we are special to Him. That makes us strong in Him. Each one of us individually has a special place in His heart, so special that Jesus died on the cross for everyone who would receive Him. This understanding should initiate a spirit of praise in each of us.

Praise, thanksgiving, and petitions

As we said earlier, we need to begin our prayer with praise and thanksgiving, acknowledging not only what God has done for us but Who He is. We can do this in quiet meditation, in verbal prayer, in song, whether modern songs, choruses, or the old favorite hymns from days gone by, and in dance as David did. But we need to be careful that the emphasis is on God, not the method or emotion.

We should pray for our family and friends. We pray for our church, our pastor and the congregation, and our own needs. But we need to be open to any other need we hear about or see, whether in our neighborhood or throughout the world. Praying for others puts us on a level to empathize with those who we don't even know personally and will probably never see. This is a part of putting others before ourselves, some of the humility that we discussed above.

I'll throw a few things out as a jumping off point for us to consider as a help in expanding our prayer lives, putting our thoughts on others, and adjusting our priorities from a "me-centered" thought pattern to a God centered prayer life.

We can pray for:

1. our president, whether we agree with him or not. Our prayers need to be for God to draw him to Himself and give him the wisdom to lead this nation according to the Light which God gives him. Every president has had his followers and his nay-sayers. But the Christian's feelings toward him personally or politically should not hinder our prayers for him. We need to pray for him to follow the will of God for the sake of our country, our kids and grandkids for many generations to come, and for the furtherance of the kingdom of God here in America.

2. our political leaders, locally, statewide, and on the national level.

    a. We can pray for their eyes to be opened so they might see the right way to lead, restoring the rights that we Christians have lost. We need to lift them up for the good of our nation and for themselves. They too are part of the "whosever" that God said could be saved. They might be as far from our political and even spiritual thoughts as the east is from the west. But at some point, east meets west and God loves them too.

    b. For those who won't follow God, that their influence will be destroyed.

3. the people of our nation to recognize the evil already here and growing and to strongly oppose it. All the evil going on around us is a symptom of a much greater evil. Remember, we wrestle not against flesh and blood but against principalities,

powers, rulers of darkness, and against spiritual wickedness. It is much deeper and more profound than wrestling against human men or women who are in power over us.

4. that our Christian brothers and sisters:

   a. will recognize our responsibility to others and our nation as a whole in social, political, and spiritual matters. God has given us a mandate to do unto others as we would have them do unto us.

   b. will understand we have the power to change the world (as every generation has wanted to do). The difference is we can bring about change because of He Who indwells us every minute of our lives. We have the power because He has given it to us IF ...

   c. will pray for God to work the desire in all Christians to get on their knees and to do it on a regular basis.

Staying focused

If you are like me as mentioned above, your mind wanders as you pray. I'll make two suggestions to help you keep on track. They aren't foolproof, but maybe you will find them helpful.

First, when you are praying alone you might consider praying out loud if you don't already do so. I don't suggest doing it in church unless you do it very quietly, under your breath, because it might be a distraction to those around you unless everyone is doing it. I find that audibly verbalizing my prayer helps me focus.

The second is to make a list of things to pray about for your personal prayer life as I mentioned above. We are sometimes prone to forget things. It may sound too regimental, but it doesn't have to be. Think of it as a tool to enhance your communion with the Lord.

Some of this may be a radical change to some of our thought processes and prayer life. But I believe it is the will of God, He Who works in us both to will and to do of His good pleasure. Remember what Paul said in Ephesians 6:12, *"For we wrestle not against flesh and blood, but against principalities, against powers, against the rulers of the darkness of this world, against spiritual wickedness in high places."*

We have seen our nation fall into a dark place. If we don't make changes in our own personal lives, our nation will fall even farther. For us to see a great reversal in the course of the good old USA, we have to have radical change in our personal and prayer lives. That's what 2 Chronicles 7:14 is all about.

Paul said in Galatians 2:20 *"I am crucified with Christ: nevertheless I live; yet not I, but Christ liveth in me: and the life which I now live in the flesh I live by the faith of the Son of God, who loved me, and gave himself for me."* I have begun to meditate on this scripture because it tells me of the strength, not of myself, but in me through Christ Who lives in me.

Interjecting 5/28/19:

I thought I had finished my final draft of *If My People* this past Saturday. Then yesterday, Monday, was Memorial Day and I asked the Lord to show me if there was something else He wanted in the book as I thought about those who had given all so we can have what we have now and enjoy the freedoms we still have.

Three things came to my mind in a short period of time. I believe they are all three a part of the type of prayer God wanted as He spoke 2 Chronicles. 7:14. They go much deeper than praying for a land or a society. They get to the heart of what God desires of His people, a way of life which some would call walking in the Spirit.

In Galatians 5:16, Paul said, "*This I say then, walk in the Spirit, and ye shall not fulfil the lust of the flesh.*" And in Romans 8:4-8 he said, "*That the righteousness of the law might be fulfilled in us, who walk not after the flesh, but after the Spirit. For they that are after the flesh do mind the things of the flesh; but they that are after the Spirit the things of the Spirit. For to be carnally minded is death; but to be spiritually minded is life and peace. Because the carnal mind is enmity against God: for it is not subject to the law of God, neither indeed can be. So then they that are in the flesh cannot please God.*"

Commitment to a personal relationship

The first thing I believe the Lord impressed on me was there are 364 days a year besides the one National Day of Prayer. What are we doing those 364 days? I'm sure there are some who are committed to praying for our nation every day. I don't know, but I imagine many, maybe most of us aren't that devoted. But I've never heard of a revival starting because of one day of prayer or a country being turned by an event which occurred on one day alone. I totally support a day being set aside but it should be only the beginning.

I went on the internet to see how long this has been going on. The National Day of Prayer website says a bill was passed on Apr. 17, 1952 for the President of the United States to set aside an appropriate day each year. A day other than Sunday was to be set aside as our National Day of Prayer.

Several things happened in ensuing years and on May 8, 1988 President Ronald Reagan signed Public Law 100-307 designating the first Thursday in May as the annual observance for the National Day of Prayer.

This shows we have had a day set aside for prayer for our nation for 67 years. And yet we as a nation are falling farther away from

God each year. What's going on? I believe this supports my belief that although this day is very important, it should be just one day out of 365 days a year when God's people are praying as they approach God in humility, seeking His face, and turning from those things we have allowed to come between us and a personal relationship with God.

I don't know when it was first stated or by whom, but there is a saying something like, "If we continue to do the same thing, we will get the same results." A specific day to pray for America is wonderful. I support it and the people who support it are to be commended. But it just isn't enough. If we Christians don't make some changes in our priorities, we will continue to see our country backslide as we watch the news. No matter what the politicians or the world think, the future is in the hands of the Christians of our nation. We will succeed IF... and only IF.

We need to advance from a single day set aside to pray for our country to being a people who are fully committed to God in the ways He requires. Then the healing of our nation will be an automatic by-product; actually, it is a promise. We American Christians need a new mindset and pure hearts. This doesn't come about by living as we have been, putting other things ahead of a deep relationship with our Heavenly Father, which amounts to idolatry.

I pray with the apostle Paul in Ephesians 3: 17-19, "*That Christ may dwell in your* (our) *hearts by faith; that ye* (we), *being rooted and grounded in love, may be able to comprehend with all saints what is the breadth, and length, and depth, and height; And to know the love of Christ, which passeth knowledge, that ye* (we) *might be filled with all the fulness of God.*" I believe many of us think and would say we live by verses 17 and 18. But when I see the last part of verse 19 I'm forced to ask myself if I am truly "filled with all the fullness of God." There are those of you who are way ahead of me. I ask you to pray for the rest of us so we also may be filled with God's fullness and begin to turn the tide for our posterity.

I urge you who are true prayer warriors to pray for those of us who are weaker in our faith and commitment. By definition, every Christian is saved and will someday be in Heaven. But too many of us are content with our position in Christ. We either do not understand the Christian life is to be ever-changing as we grow and mature in Christ or we don't want to go to the effort of transforming our lives. There is a difference in Christ as our Savior only and Christ as our Lord. There is a difference in just being saved and being a growing disciple. It is He who has saved us, but it is up to us to make Him Lord. Our position in Christ is set when we are saved, but our condition is up to us. Is our condition ever-improving, or is it stagnant?

Each one of us needs to pray for ourselves and others as Paul did in Ephesians 1:17-20, "*That the God of our Lord Jesus Christ, the Father of glory, may give unto you* (us) *the spirit of wisdom and revelation in the knowledge of him: the eyes of your* (our) *understanding being enlightened; that ye* (we) *may know what is the hope of his calling, and what* (are) *the riches of the glory of his inheritance in the saints, and what is the exceeding greatness of his power to us-ward who believe, according to the working of his mighty power, which he wrought in Christ, when he raised him from the dead, and set him at his own right hand in the heavenly places,*"

Paul and other saintly men and women throughout history have gone the extra mile though often painful and sometimes even deadly to draw closer to their Creator and Father. If we are to see our nation healed, more of us will have to join their ranks in humility as we pray and seek His face. As we do this we will more easily turn from those things that so displease our Savior. We will find as we heal spiritually our nation will be healed because of the promise given to us, God's people, in 2 Chronicles 7:14.

A clean heart

The second thing that came to my mind was a clean heart. In 1 Samuel 13, Samuel told Saul the kingdom would be taken away from him and given to a man after God's own heart. A man who the LORD had commanded to be captain over his people, speaking of David.

Then in Psalm 51:10, supposedly after David had committed adultery with Bathsheba and was called to task by Nathan, David said, "*Create in me a clean heart, O God; and renew a right spirit within me.*" I haven't sinned as David did, but this has been a sincere prayer of mine for years because I know I don't have a clean heart. I am judgmental, impatient, and struggle with pride. I've come a long way, but I need to go much farther. I want to have a heart after God's own heart.

If you have these or some other inner sin that you're struggling with, pray along with me for God to give you a clean heart. I can verify it won't happen overnight. I've thought I was a step farther than I actually was in my spiritual growth and something would happen opening my eyes to the fact I wasn't there yet. You will probably do the same; but that's a part of growth. It's in God's plan to chastise His children, so it's OK. Hebrews 12:5 & 6 says, "... *My son, despise not thou the chastening of the Lord, nor faint when thou art rebuked of him: For whom the Lord loveth he chasteneth, and scourgeth every son whom he receiveth.*"

Compassion

The third thing I believe the Lord spoke to my heart deals with compassion for lost souls and people in need. The second greatest commandment is dealt with briefly in chapter four in this book, but I believe the Lord wants to emphasize it here also.

Compassion is lacking in many of our prayers. I know it is in mine; I pray for family and friends regularly, but very rarely do I even consider those with whom I have no contact. But the lost, dying heathen in some African jungle is God's creation the same as I am. So is the pan-handler down the road.

I remember years ago we would have Missions Week and we'd pray for people in specific places. But many of us probably never gave them another thought until the next Missions Week the following year. I know we can't pray for everybody individually around the world. We can't even pray for everyone in our own community except as a group or maybe several groups. And quite honestly, my prayer alone might not make an immediate difference in the lives of most I pray for. But it can make a difference in me. God commands us to love. As I begin trying to show compassion and love for others, I believe it will actually help me fulfill the second greatest commandment in my own heart and soul. As many of us begin fulfilling this commandment, it could very well be "catching". And as we continue, it could actually make a difference in the lives of others and our nation.

There is power in your witness

Getting close to home, how many of us witness to those around us, even family and friends? I have heard it said our lives are a witness to those around us. I truly hope that is true for every Christian, but even if it is, is it enough? If I haven't already offended someone, I probably will now. Too often we use that as an excuse not to verbally witness. We don't want to hurt anyone's feelings or alienate them. I'M GUILTY! But this book isn't written for me to show you what a great example I am, because I'm not. Please understand that the words here, no matter how harsh, are the Spirit of God speaking through a man with faults and shortcomings to every reader who picks this book up.

If I truly love my family and friends, I want them to spend eternity with me in Heaven. Fulfilling the second greatest commandment requires being a witness verbally. Loving someone requires me to do the best thing I can for them. I'm beating myself up here, but God is requiring me to.

There are different books and teachings on witnessing and many make us uncomfortable because they require us to get out of our comfort zone. I just encourage you to ask the Lord to help you in your effort to do what He commands.

I hope I have clearly described how humility and prayer are vital parts of a life devoted to the Lord and that His word shows how He will respond and reward us. Prayer is closely intertwined with the third directive, to seek His face.

CHAPTER 6

And Seek My Face

★ ★ ★ ★

We should approach God in humility because of Who He is and who we are not. We *enter into his gates with thanksgiving, and into his courts with praise:...* (Psalm 100:4). This is the most important aspect of prayer. Secondarily, our Father also gives us the opportunity and encourages us to bring Him petitions for others and ourselves as part of prayer. Unfortunately, we often put more emphasis on ourselves and others than we do on God. Too many times we think of Him as the Great Giver rather than Creator, Lord, and Savior.

We know that He is the Creator. We know that Jesus, God Incarnate, is our one and only Savior, but sometimes many of us in this country have so much and need so little that we don't appreciate Him deep down. It's sort of like we sometimes acknowledge Him. He's out there, somewhere, but often or maybe even usually out of touch. But as we grow in our prayer lives, we begin to see the focus of our prayers in a different light.

We begin to seek Him in a much deeper way. It becomes not a matter of the things we do or don't do, but the life we live in Him. Many years ago an elderly lady in our church regularly talked about "practicing the presence of Jesus". She was an inspiration to all of us who desired a closer walk with the Lord. I desired what she had but had little understanding of how to get it.

I have known manly men who loved Jesus so much that tears would come to their eyes when they spoke of their love for Him. I have prayed many times that the Lord would help me love Him that much. I have prayed that I could cry for Him. I am seeking His face. Deuteronomy 4:29 says, "*But if from thence thou shalt seek the LORD thy God, thou shalt find him, if thou seek him with all thy heart and with all thy soul.*" 1 Chronicles 16:10, 11 reads, "*Glory ye in his holy name: let the heart of them rejoice that seek the LORD. Seek the LORD and his strength, seek his face continually.*"

There are some key phrases and words in these verses for those of us who desire more of Him: "**if**", "**with all thy heart**", "all thy soul", "Glory", "rejoice", and "**continually**"!

There's that "if" word again. It seems to be constantly popping up. In this case it connects seeking to finding. Without our seeking, we will not find the relationship that is available to we who are called Christians; we who are the only beings who have the opportunity to live in His presence daily, even constantly if we so desire.

We need to really understand: the seeking cannot be occasional or with little effort if we want to grow in Him. It must be wholehearted, deep down in our very souls. God has marvelous spiritual blessings that we cannot imagine on a human level, but we must want Him more than the blessings. More importantly, we must want **Him** more than anything or anyone else. As we've said before, God desires a life committed to Him in each of His people. We need to ask ourselves, "Do I desire Him that much?"

He wants us to glory and rejoice in His name. His is the name above all names; it is to be hallowed, not lightly esteemed. And the seeking must be continual if we are to be successful in finding the joy, peace, and love that come only from Him. It cannot be an on again and off again affair. We were created by God to worship and adore Him. To do any less is to miss out on the best life we can have on this earth. He forgives us for not giving our best, but we really miss out.

Growing beyond salvation

If we have received Christ as our Savior, we are heaven bound for eternity. But there is so much more for us on this earth and rewards in heaven if we go beyond the elementary teachings of salvation. The writer of Hebrews tells us in chapter 6, verses 1, 2: *"Therefore leaving the principles of the doctrine of Christ, let us go on unto perfection; not laying again the foundation of repentance from dead works, and of faith toward God, of the doctrine of baptisms, and of laying on of hands, and of resurrection of the dead, and of eternal judgment."*

Salvation is the most important possession a person can have. But that's just the beginning. God wants us to go on and on and on, continually drawing closer to Him.

Many Christians are no farther along in their walk than they were 10 or 20 or more years ago. I'm not questioning their salvation. I just wish they could understand how much more is in store for them if they would wholeheartedly commit their lives to truly seeking God.

A hymn I grew up singing was "Have Thine Own Way, Lord". I guess I've sung it hundreds of times and still love it to this day. The first verse is:

Have Thine own way, Lord,
Have Thine own way;
Thou art the Potter,
I am the clay.
Mould me and make me
After Thy will,

<blockquote>
While I am waiting,
Yielded and still.
</blockquote>

That is so beautiful and moving to me. It speaks to abiding in Him and seeking His way which I will tell you without hesitation is what I want for myself, my family, my friends, and those of you who I will never know. But that word "while" is sort of like "if" and links the first part of the verse to "waiting, yielded, and still". I want the Lord to have His way in me. I want to be the clay in the Potter's hand. But for this to happen, I have to be waiting; I have to be yielded; and I have to be still.

That is so hard for me. I need to be doing something all the time. If it's not physical it's mental. My mind is constantly on the go. I can be still physically, but it's very difficult for me to be still in my thoughts. Are you like that? If so, I think the answer for us is to learn to abide in Him. We are where we abide. If I abide in the things of the world that's where my heart is; not in tune with the things of God.

In John 15:4, Jesus said, "*Abide in me, and I in you. As the branch cannot bear fruit of itself, except it abide in the vine; no more can ye, except ye abide in me.*" I truly believe God will heal this nation if we Christians learn to abide in Jesus rather than just trying to meet with Him at certain times; sometimes; oftentimes feeling that we are in a one sided conversation.

Seeking the Face of God

Why did God say "seek My *face*". Why didn't he just say, "seek Me"? I had never thought about this until I had finished my first draft of this book and went back over it. Either way would have had the same meaning.

But I think it was to put greater emphasis on the person of God. You know what I mean if I say I'm seeking God. But if I say "I'm seeking the face of God", I believe it shows I'm seeking God with a deeper

desire than usual. God wants our very best in every way for our benefit. He has all He needs but we don't.

In translations of scripture and in our daily conversation we use
words that may not be exactly accurate, but they give emphasis to a
certain thing. When the weather is 95 degrees outside we might say
"It's hotter than blue blazes." It's a figure of speech that is obviously
not true, but it gives greater emphasis than if we just said, "It sure is
hot outside today."

Scripture says no man can see the face of God and live: "*And
he said, Thou canst not see my face: for there shall no man see me,
and live.*" Ex. 33:20

The following verses talk about seeing the face of God to describe
a great event. We need to remember that God is not a man. He is Spirit.
But since we cannot comprehend the very essence of spirit, we need
to relate in human terms so we can understand.

After Jacob wrestled with an angel for a long time during the night,
scripture says in Genesis 32:30, "*And Jacob called the name of the
place Peniel: for I have seen God face to face, and my life is preserved.*"
I've never wrestled with an angel, but if I did, I'm sure I'd describe
the event much more emphatically than I would have a school play-
ground brawl. Also, if God did wrestle with any man, I don't think the
man would last through the first round, especially not until daylight.

Exodus 33:9-11 says, "*And it came to pass, as Moses entered into
the tabernacle, the cloudy pillar descended, and stood at the door of
the tabernacle, and the LORD talked with Moses. And all the people
saw the cloudy pillar stand at the tabernacle door: and all the people
rose up and worshipped, every man in his tent door. And the LORD
spake unto Moses face to face, as a man speaketh unto his friend.*"
This had to be an awesome experience that needed special emphasis.
If you envisioned yourself as you prayed as speaking face to face with
God, however you picture Him, don't you imagine it would give you a

greater depth in your prayer life? If you don't already, I'd encourage you to try it. You'll like it.

In Deuteronomy 5: 1-6 Moses talked to the people of Israel and said in vs. 4, "*The LORD talked with you face to face in the mount out of the midst of the fire*". We know this was a figure of speech because in v. 5 Moses said, "*(I stood between the LORD and you at that time, to shew you the word of the LORD: for ye were afraid by reason of the fire, and went not up into the mount;)*". The people were afraid of the Lord and certainly would not look at His face, even if they could.

"Face to face" is a figure of speech to emphasize the importance of communing with God. The words God and god are used so often and in various ways that the world has become insensitive to the name of God. I believe He knew that would happen and that's why He used the word "face".

Here's another thought that may be of benefit to us as we seek His face. As we commune with God in prayer we speak directly to Him. But a lot of our songs and hymns are *about* Him. There is nothing wrong with that, but if we intentionally personalize our time of worship, I think it helps us draw closer to Him. For instance, rather than singing, "He is Lord" try singing "You are Lord." "He has risen from the dead and He is Lord" might have more meaning to us personally if we change it just a little to sing *to* Him rather than *about* Him. Singing "You are risen from the dead and You are Lord" might help us feel more like we are in His presence.

Meditation is another thing that will help us as we seek His face. Meditation is not a bad word. We have heard of it being used in non-Christian religions and the word has received a bad rap. But we can meditate on scripture, slowly repeating it over and over in our minds, allowing it to become a part of our thought process. We can also meditate on the person of God (or Jesus). In doing so, we can turn all our thoughts toward Him.

If you don't already meditate, you might consider incorporating it into your prayer life. You can find Christian books that teach meditation, just stay away from non-Christian meditation for spiritual purposes. Spiritual meditation is more than controlling the mind. It does have an aspect of that, trying to block other things out of our minds, but its purpose is to focus on our Creator, Father, and Lord. Meditation can be developed as we practice it.

Please! Seek the face of God! Personalize your prayer life in a way you may never have before. Remember, truly seeking the face of God should not be an occasional effort. It should be and can be a continual way of life.

CHAPTER 7

And Turn from Their Wicked Ways

* * *

I must interject before I go any further that I just realized it may seem I give little credence to Christians of other nations. Please forgive me if that is how you have taken my writing about America. God loves every Christian of every country just as much as He loves Christians in America. The healing I'm saying can be accomplished in America can be accomplished in any nation where God the Father, Son, and Holy Spirit are lifted up by His people, Christians who love God enough to humble themselves before Him, pray, seek His face, and turn from their wicked ways. What I am writing to my fellow Americans can be used by Christians throughout the world to receive healing for their land.

We need to understand what God means by "wicked ways" as they pertain to His people, specifically in this writing, American Christians today. There are sins of "commission", the bad things we do but should not; and there are sins of "omission", the good things we should do but don't. We have heard the word "sin" so many times that it doesn't always mean anything to us. We have become insensitive to it. But

God uses the word "wicked" which sounds harsher. What might be trivial to us just may be wicked to God.

Just a few synonyms of wicked on the internet are: evil, sinful, immoral, wrong, morally wrong, wrongful, bad, iniquitous, corrupt, base, mean, and vile. If you think what I'm about to say is going off the deep end, remember what Isaiah 55:8, 9 says, *"For my thoughts are not your thoughts, neither are your ways my ways, saith the LORD. For as the heavens are higher than the earth, so are my ways higher than your ways, and my thoughts than your thoughts."*

Just maybe those "little" things we do wrong or don't do but should are actually wicked in the eyes of God. That just doesn't sound fair does it? God knows we all sin to one degree or another; we can't seem to help it. So why would He use such strong language when I make a mistake?

The point of 2 Chronicles 7:14 goes deeper than the act itself. Yes, sin is wrong, even wicked in the eyes of God. But Christians are forgiven. I will never be without sin and God knows it. But He forgives me when I repent. This scripture, I believe, is speaking of a way of life; a person's intentions and purposes in life, his very heart. It says, *"turn from their wicked ways"*. This implies that some of His people are consistently behaving in ways in which He disapproves. To really understand God's word to us today, I think the emphasis should be on the word "ways". And let us not make the mistake of looking at this from our own perspectives that have probably been dulled over the years. Let's try to look as much as we can from God's perspective.

Looking at things from God's perspective

David sinned greatly as king but Samuel had said of David as he spoke to King Saul in 1 Samuel 13:14, *"But now thy kingdom* (Saul's) *shall not continue: the LORD hath sought him a man after his own heart, and the LORD hath commanded him* (David) *to be captain over his people, because thou hast not kept that which the LORD commanded thee.*" Although David committed sins as an imperfect man, more vile sins than most of us have committed, his heart was toward God so God gave him favor. Even so, we can't use David as an excuse for us to live a life unpleasing to God.

There is something we need to remember; David did not have the Holy Spirit to guide him 24/7 as we do. In the Old Testament, God sometimes put His Spirit on an individual for a specific purpose or for a period of time. The Holy Spirit didn't indwell them as He does us now. Since the ascension of Christ, the Spirit of God indwells every saved person, every man and woman; every child, teenager, and adult; you and even me! The simple act of recognizing the FACT that the Spirit of God indwells us can help us realize that the power to live and walk in the Spirit more actively and effectively is possible for us. I'm not saying it's easy, but it is possible and we should begin acknowledging this and meditating on it daily. As the Holy Spirit becomes more dominant in our thoughts and actions; as we begin to understand that the overcoming power of the Holy Spirit within us knows the mind of God because He is a part of the Trinity; we will begin to delight in the Lord and be more pleasing to Him.

Psalm 37:4 "*Delight thyself also in the LORD; and he shall give thee the desires of thine heart.*" Do we truly delight in the Lord? Or do we delight in the pleasures of our lives that have nothing to do with God? The pleasures themselves may not be wrong or immoral, but our making them a bigger part of our lives than God is one of the "wicked ways" that sorely displeases God. This is because they replace Him as number one in our lives. Can we really expect God to give us this type of desire?

We often think "*he shall give thee the desires of thine heart*" means He will give us those things we are currently desiring. That could very well be if we have first delighted in the Lord. If we have truly delighted in Him our desires will be in accord with His will. They won't be the base desires of the flesh common to man.

I personally think this is a two-step process. First, if I delight in Him, He will place (put in me) those desires in my heart that He wants me to have. Secondly, then and only then, He will allow those desires to come about at the proper time. We must realize His timing may be different than ours.

Being of great price in the sight of God is the opposite of the wicked ways He speaks of in the scripture. 1 Peter 3:4 says, "*But let it be the hidden man of the heart, in that which is not corruptible, even the ornament of a meek and quiet spirit, which is in the sight of God of great price.*" I must ask myself, "Does God consider my hidden man to be an ornament of great price?

Evaluate your standing in His sight

I believe there are several barometers we could consider to determine where we individually stand in the sight of God.

Possibly the most obvious are the fruit of the Spirit; *love, joy, peace, longsuffering* (patience), *gentleness, goodness, faith, meekness, and temperance* (self-control). Galatians 5:22. These are the attributes of the man whose heart is in tune with God. They are called fruit because they develop and grow as we grow in our relationships with the Spirit Who indwells us. Our positive response to the leading of the Holy Spirit is the nourishment needed for the fruit to grow to maturity.

Jesus said in John 15: 4-6, "*Abide in me, and I in you. As the branch cannot bear fruit of itself, except it abide in the vine; no more can ye, except ye abide in me. I am the vine, ye are the branches: He that abideth in me, and I in him, the same bringeth forth much fruit: for without me ye can do nothing. If a man abide not in me, he is cast forth as a branch, and is withered; and men gather them, and cast them into the fire, and they are burned."*

I have a lot of green, un-ripened fruit but I am endeavoring to respond to the workings of the Lord in me so those green fruit will ripen. I pray I will be able to respond so much that they ripen and fall from me, blessing those around me. However much of these you see in me will give you an idea of whether I'm delighting in the Lord. I believe that is true of all of us. Each one of these fruit could be a study in itself, but this isn't the place for it right now.

But I will speak briefly on the first one, love. Love is the first fruit mentioned and could be thought of as the basis for all the rest of the fruit. Without love we might be happy to a degree at different times, but I don't think we could experience real joy or peace. Without love I seriously doubt that I could be patient, meek, gentle, good, or have much temperance (self-control) with someone that opposed me, my family or friends, or even just my thoughts.

Some modern translations use the word faithful or faithfulness rather than faith. Whichever is most correct, I can't have much faith in God if I don't love Him and I probably won't be very faithful to Him or another person if I don't have love for them.

Love enables us

When asked what the greatest commandment was, Jesus quoted Deuteronomy 6:5, replying in Matthew 22:37, *"Thou shalt love the Lord thy God with all thy heart, and with all thy soul, and with all thy mind. This is the first and great commandment. And the second is like unto it, Thou shalt love thy neighbour as thyself. On these two commandments hang all the law and the prophets."* Having the love of God within us gives us the ability to obey the commandments. We cannot have the love of God and revel in "wicked ways". So the question is, "Do I have the love of God within me?" Not does God love me, but do I truly love God and others as He has commanded?

But why would God command us to love? We fall in love with someone as if we have no control over our feelings. We can't help it. We can't not love them. It just happens. We love our parents, siblings, and best friends just because we do. We love them despite disagreements and even quarrels. When that brand new baby makes its' debut, we immediately love him or her. It's just natural. And we can love God, at least we think we do, because He loves us and is our Creator.

But how can I love the unlovely, or the guy that I can't stand to be around, or someone of another race, country, or religion that is totally opposite from mine? Why would God command me to love these people? He can command me to love because He is love and He wants the best for me spiritually that I can attain with His help. I may never be as spiritually mature as He desires me to be; I may not reach my own potential; but I can certainly grow from where I am now.

The question then is not how can He command me to do what is seemingly impossible, but how can I do what He commands? I can't on my own, not by myself. We must go back to Philippians 2:13 "*For it is God which worketh in you both to will and to do of his good pleasure.*" I cannot in the flesh love some people. There is absolutely no way! Here is where the "rubber meets the road".

2 Corinthians 5:17 says, "*Therefore if any man be in Christ, he is a new creature: old things are passed away; behold, all things are become new.*" So what has become new? That unlovable guy isn't any different. He hasn't become new. This scripture says that if I am in Christ, which I am because I have received Him as my Savior, it is me that is a new creature. Now that I have received Christ, I need to receive what He has given me. He has given me a new life and a new way of thinking. But it's not that easy is it? We need to go back to Galatians 2:20 to re-enforce this new revelation. It says, "*I am cruci-*

fied with Christ: nevertheless I live; yet not I, but Christ liveth in me: and the life which I now live in the flesh I live by the faith of the Son of God, who loved me, and gave himself for me."

Yes, there are some people I just cannot make myself love. But that's the thing. I can't do it! It must be Christ living in me that enables me to love. In order to do this, I have to regularly remind myself that I am not the old me. Christ has given me a new life in Him. But I must appropriate it. I must lay hold of it or it is nothing to me.

This is another place where I personally use visualization to help my self-seeking mind be replaced by the Spirit of God. He is right here in me waiting for me to let Him be my Helper. If I can visualize or recognize that Christ died for that man the same as He died for me because He loves him as much as He loves me, it enables me to see that man in a totally different light. I can begin to see him as God sees him, a living, imperfect human being with a soul and a spirit, just like me.

Completing our discussion of love we should look at what Jesus said in John 13:35; *By this shall all men know that ye are my disciples, if ye have love one to another.* When people look at us, they should be able to see a difference from what they see and experience in the world of the flesh.

I began this chapter talking about turning from our wicked ways. It may seem that I've gone off on a tangent talking about love, but love is the thing that allows us to turn from those wicked ways. Think about it. What are wicked ways? They are things we do against God and other people. But if we have the love God commands, the two greatest commandments according to Christ, we won't have those wicked ways as a part of our lives.

Unfortunately, there are some other barometers that can be used to see where we Christians stand in our relationship with God. Hatred, unforgiveness, prejudice, abusiveness, constant anger, even lying, impatience, and lack of self-control are also fruit. But they are not fruit of the Holy Spirit. They are fruit of the flesh, used by Satan in the lives of immature Christians to inhibit spiritual growth. Yes, these are often fruit possessed by Christians, people who have been saved by grace; going to spend eternity in heaven; yet missing out on the abundant life that God has for those of us who will truly seek it.

I must admit: impatience and lack of self-control, along with pride, have held me back for years. I am a Christian, I'm heaven bound, and I'm maturing in my Christian walk. But I could have been a lot farther down the path of sanctification if I had allowed the Holy Spirit to work these things out of me many years ago. These things have hindered me from being the Christian that could apply 2 Chronicles 7:14 to my daily life.

I doubt I'm the only Christian who has this rotten fruit in my life. Do you have some level of one or more of these fruit spoiling the branch? If so, humble yourselves before God; ask Him to forgive you and repent. Turn away from these things in the power of the abiding Holy Spirit within you. You can begin by constantly reminding yourself, *"I can do all things through Christ which strengtheneth me"*. Philippians 4:13. A leopard cannot change his spots. Neither can you become a new man or woman on your own. It can be done only by Christ in you.

When you are tempted or even fall, remember what Paul said above in Galatians 2:20, *"I am crucified with Christ: nevertheless I live; yet not I, but Christ liveth in me: and the life which I now live in the flesh I live by the faith of the Son of God, who loved me, and gave himself for me."*

This whole chapter could be summed up as follows: If God is first in my life, before anyone or anything else, sin will be overcome by loving Him. Sin is the symptom of a life apart from God.

Turning from our wicked ways is the last of the requirements God gave in order for us to receive personal forgiveness and for our nation to be healed. The scriptures in these last four chapters should have pricked our hearts and caused us to want to be obedient to 2 Chronicles 7:14. But after all, we are human. We have most likely forgotten at least some of the thoughts, if not most, that came to us over the last few weeks as we read, contemplated, and tried to make these scriptures a part of our lives.

But I encourage you, don't let these scriptures be like a lot of books we have read or thoughts of improvement that were quickly gone from our minds. They may have had an impression on us as we read them. But most things I have read and intentions I've had for spiritual growth haven't quickly become a part of my life. If they had, I would be a much stronger Christian than I am now. The good fruit would be plentiful in my life, evident to all around me.

Whether you remember or keep the words I have written on these pages or not, keep the scriptures where you can go back over them regularly. Let them penetrate your very soul. Just reading this book or memorizing 2 Chronicles 7:14 will not get us closer to God's forgiveness and healing. It will have just been another exercise of futility.

We must take control of every phase of our lives and draw nearer to God. When the Christians of this great country unite in spirit to seek our God's face and all He requires we will see the next chapter come into being. I believe it will be a national revival like we've never experienced or read about.

The following excerpt is from NDR's email dated 12/20/19 entitled "Fruit for Christmas".

During the Christmas season years ago, in December 1973, in the midst of the Watergate scandal, one United States Senator from Oregon, Mark Hatfield, knew the power of Scripture and American

Christian history. When the nation was getting more and more divided he had the boldness to seek to bring the fruit of God's Presence not just to family and neighbors but to the whole American nation. He introduced and had passed unanimously by voice vote a key spiritual "weapon."

Like Lincoln in the Civil War he called for a National Day of Humiliation, Fasting and Prayer. Using many of President Lincoln's words, all of which speak to us today, Senator Hatfield called upon Scripture to bring about God's Presence to the nation for His healing. Part of the text reads: *"it is the duty of nations, as well as of men to owe their dependence upon the overruling power of God, to confess their sins and transgressions, in humble sorrow, yet with assured hope that genuine repentance will lead to mercy and pardon, and to recognize the sublime truth, announced in the Holy Scriptures and proven by all history, that those nations are blessed whose God is Lord... We have been preserved these many years in peace and prosperity. We have grown in numbers, wealth and power as no other nation has ever grown. But we have forgotten God; we have forgotten the gracious hand which preserved us in peace, and multiplied and enriched us; and we have vainly imagined, in the deceitfulness of our hearts, that all these blessings were produced by some superior wisdom and virtue of our own. Intoxicated with unbroken success, we have become too self-sufficient to feel the necessity of redeeming and preserving grace, too proud to pray to the God that made us! It behooves us, then, to humble ourselves before the offended Power, to confess our national sins, and to pray for clemency and forgiveness......"*

Can we agree that the nation needs healing? Question: why aren't our "leaders" following God's time-tested Solution to heal a nation today?

Our forefathers knew this key spiritual strategy; by 1815 there had been almost eight hundred times that church or political leaders in the colonies or the new nation called for a Day of Humiliation, Fasting and Prayer. Wars and plagues were avoided. The nation was blessed each time.

2 Chronicles 7:14 says:

" *...if My people who are called by My name will humble themselves, and pray and seek My face, and turn from their wicked ways, THEN I will hear from heaven, and will forgive their sin and heal their land.*"(emphasis supplied)

What can you and I do? We can write the President and our members of Congress urging them to call for a Day of Humiliation, Fasting and Prayer. Also we, at the grassroots, can take up repentance as a daily practice, beginning to cleanse as His Bride. And we can continue to pray for our leaders as Scripture tells us in 1 Timothy 2:1-4: *Therefore I exhort first of all that supplications, prayers, intercessions, and giving of thanks be made for all men, for kings and all who are in authority, that we may lead a quiet and peaceable life in all godliness and reverence. For this is good and acceptable in the sight of God our Savior, who desires all men to be saved and to come to the knowledge of the truth.*

As you and I pray for "all who are in authority" may the Lord touch the President or a member of Congress to speak a "Senator Hatfield" solution for this divided nation.

The nation can use that type of Good Fruit for Christmas.

Permission to use this was granted by Jeff Daly, founder and director of National Day of Repentance. I would encourage you to look at the NDR website and sign up for Jeff's emails concerning repentance for personal, national, and worldwide repentance. It is www.repentday.com. His email address is pastorjeff@repentday.com. I have said several times in this book that one day of national prayer is not enough to restore our nation. Neither is one day of repentance. But it's a beginning. NDR's emphasis is on continual repentance, turning from our wicked ways of ignoring our Creator God. In Jeff's mind, every day is repent day.

May the Spirit of God in you be evident to you as you live out each day for the rest of your lives. *If we live in the Spirit, let us also walk in the Spirit.*Galatians 5:25

CHAPTER 8

Then Will I Hear from Heaven

★ ★ ★ ★

THEN! That's the word that always follows "IF", either literally, or implied. The promise given after the word "then" will not happen without the instructions following "if" being met. IF we, God's people, will humble ourselves, pray, seek His face, and turn from our wicked ways, THEN He will hear us and ---. It obviously takes all four requirements, not just the ones that are easy for us. If we could pick just one or the ones we like, He would have told us.

Doesn't He always hear us? He obviously knows everything we say and think. But I believe this scripture speaks about something other than physically hearing an audible voice in prayer with the ears or knowing the silent petition of the mind. I think there are a LOT of prayers we Christians make that God allows to go in one ear and out the other. I often think about Christian parents praying that their child's team will win the next football game. Many of us have done that with no malice intended toward the other team. We just love our kids and want to see them succeed in every endeavor they pursue. But what is God to do when an equally spiritual parent from the other team utters the same prayer for his child's team? Should He make it a tie so no-one will be defeated? I'm sure there would be a lot of no-win games played across the country. No-one would lose, but the prayer still hasn't been answered the way the Christian parents prayed.

That may seem irrelevant to our topic and maybe even a little ridiculous. But the point is that God must answer prayer according to His overall plan for His people, a lot of which we will never understand, and according to Who He is. Although the Friday night game is important to our kids and therefore important to us, it usually has little if anything to do with spiritual maturity.

Back on topic: God's desire for each of us is to diligently pursue spiritual maturity. Spiritual maturity involves much more than prayer, although it is a vital part of the Christian walk and I do not mean to trivialize it.

We might more easily understand if the word "respond" had been used rather than "hear". In other words, "then will I 'respond' from heaven". I'm not trying to rewrite the words God spoke. I'm merely putting His intended meaning into words I believe we can more easily understand. It's no different than one Bible scholar translating the original Hebrew or Greek into the KJV while others have translated the original into the NIV, ESV, NASB or one of the other translations using different words to get the point across. I have not changed the meaning. I have only clarified it for our modern day understanding.

Why would God not respond to some prayers? Because He cannot be other than Who He is.

I'm going to do something I normally do not like and would do only if it would still be true and serve a very important purpose. I'm going to take a scripture out of context. Paul said in 2 Corinthians 6:14, "— *for what fellowship hath righteousness with unrighteousness? And what communion hath light with darkness?*" It's out of context because Paul was talking about believers being unequally yoked with unbelievers. But it is just as relevant to God (light) not responding to every prayer of people who have been saved but who have not fully submitted themselves to the Father of lights and thereby being in darkness in their understanding. This is because He has a purpose for their lives that goes deeper than they can ever imagine.

The change we seek starts with our individual obedience

James 5:16(b) says, "*The effectual fervent prayer of a righteous man availeth much.*" This seems to imply that a quick, desperate prayer of one who has not dedicated his life to knowing God and His will for his life will not avail much. Who is the righteous man James is talking about? One who is in right standing with God although not without fault; one who is saved and constantly, diligently seeking more of God, not just every now and then when a need arises. We talked about positional righteousness and relational righteousness earlier. We need to understand that the context of this discussion now is relational, not positional.

Has God ever not answered my prayers the way I expected? You'd better believe it! Many times! But I am confident that as I seek more of Him, to be more like Jesus, I will walk in the Spirit more and more every day. I must strive to walk in the Spirit even when I do not feel spiritual, which is the case more often than I care to admit. Then my prayers will be more in line with His will and therefore be answered more often as I ask them.

So I must ask myself, "What must I, an imperfect man, do to be righteous in God's eyes and see more of my prayers answered?" Maybe a little encouragement is needed at this point for me to seek righteousness.

David committed adultery and murder and yet God said he was a man after His own heart. David was devoted to God and God was devoted to David. God supplied him with great wealth and success. He was so important to God that many of the Old Testament people were referred to as descendants of David, all the way to Jesus.

The act of committing a sin is obviously wrong in God's eyes. But more important to God than the act is the intent of the heart that preceded the act. God will forgive the act of sin committed by a Christian, but if the heart isn't changed similar acts of sin will continue in a vicious cycle. David's acts of adultery and murder were wrong. But, more importantly, they were committed because his heart had wandered from being God-centered to self-centered. He was therefore not allowed to build God's temple, something he had greatly desired to do.

In an effort to be righteous I could list the Ten Commandments and sincerely purpose in my heart to follow them as much as is humanly possible. I could list numerous sins that God detests such as lying, gossiping, un-forgiveness, jealousy, pride, and on and on and determine in my heart that I would not commit them. All this is good and I believe most Christians try to live by these standards. Unfortunately, our nation is still headed to destruction, both physically and spiritually if something doesn't change. So what's the problem?

We must go back to the first part of the verse, the IF's.

- Are we as the body of Christ humbling ourselves before God? Or are we seeking our own way, putting other things before a deeper relationship with God?
- Is the body of Christ as a whole truly praying as we know we should? Is our prayer life consistent? Are we regularly entering His gates with thanksgiving and into His courts with praise? Or are we usually listing our needs and desires, asking

that they be accomplished? And that only as our conscience dictates or as needed?

- Are we seeking His face? Are we desiring to be one with the Father and the Son? Do we recognize that we are the temple of God? Do we live like the Spirit of God actually dwells within us, which He does? Do we even know what all that means? Or is it nothing more than pie in the sky that we don't think we can ever attain to as mortal human beings?

- Have we turned from our wicked ways? Or are we still trying to fulfill those self-centered desires, putting our momentary pleasures before a deeper relationship with God? That will keep us at arm's length from a deep walk with our Creator.

Only as we seriously consider and act on these four requirements God put before us will we see our nation turned around. He has put the responsibility squarely on the shoulders of His people, Christians whether Jew or Gentile. He hasn't put it on the political system. He hasn't put it on charity groups. He hasn't put it on the Pope who Christians and non-Christians alike look up to. He hasn't even put the responsibility to turn this nation around on the most powerful man in the world, POTUS, the president of the United States.

He has put the responsibility to go from IF to THEN on each of us little Christians, no matter how insignificant we may be in the eyes of the world. All of us together are the bride of Christ. All of us little people can together have the opportunity to see this USA become a God-fearing nation again. We can see God allowed to be in places where He is no longer allowed to even be spoken of.

The future of our children and grandchildren is up to us.

CHAPTER 9

And Will Forgive Their Sin and Will Heal Their Land.

★ ★ ★ ★

In the previous chapters, we have seen the cure for the sinful slump this great land has fallen into. God has the power to do anything He wants to. The God Who is powerful enough to make the universe and everything in it doesn't need help to do anything. He created the world and He can fix it. He could fix our country by Himself. But He has chosen His people, you and me and our brothers and sisters in Christ to begin the work, to take the first steps.

In the past we have fallen short in fulfilling our responsibility to God. Now we've seen what we can do. Not only can we, but we must. We must humble ourselves before our great Creator. We must pray more and seek His face. We must repent, turning from our wicked ways to a commitment to our Heavenly Father to do His will. It isn't an easy task, but if God requires it, He will provide the strength and fortitude to submit to His authority. Part of our prayer needs to be asking Him for the strength and guidance to do what we know we must.

When we have done as He requires we have fulfilled our responsibility as explained in 2 Chronicles 7:14. Now we can begin seeing the results we've been waiting and praying for.

Note that the first thing God promises is that He will forgive us of our sin. We've probably all been concentrating on the healing of our land. But God's greatest concern is the sin that has caused us to be in the predicament we're in now. That sin was putting other things in the place of God. He said in Exodus 20:3, "*Thou shalt have no other gods before me.*" When we put other things or people before God we are guilty of idol worship. Idols are not restricted to little graven images or totem poles. An idol can be anything or anyone that causes us to take our eyes off God and put them on something that has no benefit beyond our time here on earth. The degradation of morality and increase in crime throughout history have been symptoms of a declining spiritual condition running rampant. Hopefully, this is a part of each of our own personal histories, gone forever as we repent individually and for our nation so we may receive His forgiveness.

God has promised not only to forgive each of us of our great and terrible sin, but to go a step further and heal our nation. The sin of our nation started us on a wide, dark, and ugly path. Now the repentance of His people in our nation will reverse our course and put us back on the narrow path of righteousness and healing.

Looking to the future

Assuming God has removed the scales from our eyes and we're committed to Him, He will begin making this country what it once was, even better. This endeavor has been a laborious journey, not without struggle and hardship. During the process, we humbled ourselves before God and submitted to His Lordship, putting Him before our jobs, hobbies, and even our families. We Christians have always said God is first in our lives; now we've proven it.

We've prayed more often, longer, and with more fervency than we ever thought possible.

We've been on our knees, seeking His face; longing to love and fear Him more; taking hold of that one-ness with Him that has evaded us for so long.

We have seen that the things we do, our lifestyles, were grievous to our Father. We've repented and turned from those things we thought were OK and innocent, realizing they were wicked in the eyes of the Creator of the universe because we were putting them before our Maker and Redeemer.

It hasn't happened overnight. But as the title of this chapter ends with a period, so does this part of our journey. Although the journey of transformation only ends at death, the hard part is in the past. It is history. The future will be a continuance and reinforcement of what we have learned. And if (there's that word again) we continue to follow the guidelines, the answer will be ours. Forgiveness of our sin and healing of this great land of America will belong to us. We can rightfully say once again "We live in the home of the free and the land of the brave" because we have stood against Satan and his schemes, the smoke-screen of politics and evil. We have fought the good fight. We are children of God and joint heirs with Christ in the greatest nation that has ever existed.

When God gives us an "if" and "then", it is an agreement that He will not break. If we have performed our part of the agreement, He will gladly do His part. We can rest assured that He will not forget His promise.

Our part of the deal has been completed and the promise will be "signed and delivered" by our Father. But we must not give up hope when our healing doesn't happen overnight. Hebrews 11:1 says,

"*Now faith* is the substance of things *hoped for, the evidence of things not seen.* When we've done our part our faith that God will do His part will be the evidence to us that He will. God's timing is His business. Our continued faith that He will do as He said will be the substance that will cause the healing to come about. It may be a long process, but it will happen; maybe gradually. The important thing is while we are waiting on God, we will be growing in our relationships with Him because of what He has shown us in His Word.

I pray every Christian who reads this book will take 2 Chronicles 7:14 to heart and remember that each one of us may be insignificant on our own, but many of us standing against the wiles of the devil can cause America to change course. We can once again be called a God-fearing nation, a nation under God. We can have prayer in our schools and public places without harassment. We can see the Bible revered as much more than a dust collector on the coffee table. We can once again see civility in places where it has been missing for a long time.

I pray also that every non-Christian who has read this will understand who God is and that He wants them to come into the fold through faith in the Lamb without blemish, Jesus Christ, the Son of God.

God is not only Lord and Savior to Christians, but He will be the Savior to our once again great country, greater than it has ever been. This is not intended to be a political statement. It's a statement by a Christian who knows that greatness is ultimately in the hands of God the Father, Son, and Holy Spirit. He will use His people to attain His goals when we allow Him to.

This is the last chapter looking at the parts of 2 Chronicles 7:14 individually. But there are two more parts to this book. The "Conclusion" is very important, but the "Addendum" is the most important concerning the kingdom of God.

May God restore and bless the USA.

CONCLUSION

As I begin writing this morning, I want to interject something that is probably contrary to correct writing technique, but is perfectly relevant to the purpose of this book. Today is November 23, 2017, a day of Thanksgiving in America, the land in which I was born, raised, and have lived in with great freedom for seventy years. I thank God that I can write this to God-fearing believers throughout a free nation without fear of government persecution. In a few hours Diane and I will be joining our sons' family and friends for a wonderful meal in celebration of the day. My daughter and her family are out of state enjoying themselves as are tens of thousands of freedom loving Americans that can come and go as they please.

Throughout other countries of the world there is persecution and murder of Christians, government abuse, torture, and murder of their citizens, terrorism, war, and starvation. Isis and the Taliban as well as many other smaller groups are terrorizing and killing people in various countries.

News this morning talked about a North Korean soldier that escaped across the DMZ to South Korea fleeing the murderous regime. He was hit by North Korean bullets five times and lived to be pulled to safety by South Korean soldiers. He is suffering from depression, malnutrition, and parasites as the North Korean dictator is threatening nuclear war.

The Syrian government has killed thousands of its citizens, men, women, and children, in horrendous ways. These are just a few of the terrors that exist in many parts of the world. Many of our own soldiers have been killed or injured in battles trying to defend peoples and freedom throughout the world in recent years as well as in past wars. Many other young men and women have come home and suffered tragically from PTSD, some losing everything they had as well as hope, even committing suicide. We blame the governments and radical groups of individuals who have no concern for life, liberty and the pursuit of happiness of others, as we should.

But the real reason which is seldom discussed is EVIL itself. There is a devil named Satan and there is a war going on. The people committing those terrible acts are controlled by Satan whether they know it or not. There are two opposing forces in this world - evil and good. Those performing these atrocities should be punished but we Christians need to put ultimate blame on the source of all evil, Satan himself. We can't catch him, imprison him, or kill him. But we can, as a very large Christian group of evil-haters, do the bidding of the One who can and will subdue him, submitting our own individual lives to His call and purpose for us individually and as a nation.

Here in the USA:

September 11, 2001 marked the end of a time when Americans could safely assemble and just plain live without thinking they could be injured or even killed by someone with a drive for destruction influenced by foreign or even home-grown evil.

Today NYC put 2,000 more police officers than usual on their streets to guard the millions of people who will be attending the Macy's parade. They had to do this because of the terrorist attacks, both large and small, that have hit our country as well as others in preceding years.

Innocent children and those who are trying to help them grow to be mature men and women are being killed in their own schools.

Others are killed on the streets.

Law enforcement and even fire fighters are being targeted by evil.

Random individuals and groups are being mowed down by shooters and vehicle drivers.

Dominating TV and radio now are public figures, politicians, businessmen, clergy, and figures dominant in acting and the media production fields who have been found out and disgraced because of multiple sex offenses and crimes perpetrated over many years, even decades.

Our laws punish those who abuse or kill innocent animals but allow the breaking of the fifth commandment by willingly murdering unwanted, innocent, unborn human embryos and babies.

Alternate lifestyles that are contrary to scripture have become the norm in our society. Some of those things the Bible speaks against and our grandparents abhorred are now accepted as OK. Even we Christians often overlook them because there is nothing we can do about it. It often affects our own families.

All this evil in our current society, in addition to unmentioned crimes throughout history, have come to be accepted as normal in our "civilized" country. Please forgive me if I have left out a crime in which you have lost a loved one. They all need to be acknowledged.

This is nothing new. There has been conflict since Cain killed Abel. There have been wars since there were enough people to wage war. Mass murders, genocides, torture, and the holocaust are all a part of world history. But now evil is coming closer to home. It's actually here now more than we would have ever imagined. We're beginning to see it's not just something that happens overseas or in big cities or to other people.

Satan has always had an influence in the American way of life. All of us have sinned because we have succumbed to the wiles of the devil. Some have committed atrocities and there have been those other sins that are between what we call little "white lies" and mass murder. But there is something more now. Satan has gained a foothold in this great country that our forefathers would never have imagined. I'm not trying to be dramatic but it's true.

The people and groups that commit these crimes are individually responsible and should be punished to the fullest extent of the law. But we must do something more! The above atrocities and horrors will only get worse in our beloved country until and unless we, God's people, humble ourselves before our God, pray, seek His face, and turn from our wicked ways. No person in the White House, no person in congress, no police commissioner, and not even the Pope (and I say that respectfully) can turn America back into the God fearing, safe country it once was and can be again.

A couple of days ago I heard a lady on the radio whose political views are different from mine and the president's but I respect her for what she said to a listening audience of thousands. After a back and forth conversation with the interviewer she made the statement that she loves this country and prays for the country and the president. She realizes that although she disagrees with his politics, she is called upon by her God to pray for him. As I said earlier, praying for the country and its' leaders isn't the focal point of 2 Chronicles 7:14 (although it is spoken of in other scriptures), but it was encouraging to me to hear a person with clout, a politician, talking about praying on a public radio station.

(interjecting 3/23/19) I wrote above about Isis in 2017 committing horrendous atrocities. Yesterday the news reports told us their last stronghold had been taken back and they have been defeated. They no longer control any town and many have gone underground. But as I say this, we know they are still active on a smaller scale in several countries and are just waiting for the opportunity to rise again.

Also, our president has had two meetings with the North Korean leader and is hopefully making strides toward nuclear disarmament of that country. However, surveillance and intelligence reports put that statement in question.

Our economy is apparently improving and unemployment is down.

Despite these apparent improvements in world government and our own economy, I have seen no improvements in the overall spiritual state of our union. Neither have there been any significant changes worldwide. If you go back and reread the first part of this conclusion, you will see no difference now from what I wrote in 2017. Satan is still on the rampage. He will find other avenues to bring America to its knees along with the rest of the world.

I believe any improvements we see apart from our national and personal repentance will be short-lived and may only lull us into thinking we're going to be OK after all. The names of evil people and countries will change; time will move on; but without God's intervention the overall condition of our nation and the world will only get worse.

Revival

I have heard people say things like, "When are we going to get our country back?" We'll get it back from Satan's ever-tightening grip when we do the things God said would cause Him to get it back for us. He alone can do it.

It is time we Christians as a whole put God first and EVERY-THING else after Him. I pray regularly that God will give me a clean heart and I pray, submitting my thoughts, words, actions, attitude, emotions, will, desires, and very being to Him. I have not reached the maturity God or even I desire for myself. *But I press toward the mark for the prize of the high calling of God in Christ Jesus.* Philippians 3:14.

Proverbs 14:34 reads, *"Righteousness exalteth a nation: but sin is a reproach to any people."* Will you join me and tens of thousands of your American brothers and sisters in Christ as we commit to a lifestyle that is pleasing to our Father? It won't be easy, but it will be worth it; not only to you and me, but to our children, grandchildren, and their children and grandchildren who we will never know, but who will reap the benefits of what we have sown.

It is my hope and prayer that the words and especially scriptures in this book will convince many of God's people to take up the cross for the sake of our great land and submit to the hope God gave us in 2 Chronicles 7:14. But I am not naive enough to think that all readers will.

Jesus gave the parable of the sower in Matthew 13. In brief, some seeds fell by the wayside, some on stony places, some among thorns, and some on good ground. In Christ's explanation of the parable He likened the seed that fell by the wayside to people who didn't understand the word and Satan took away the little that entered their hearts. The seeds which fell on stony places are like a man who joyfully received the word but when troubles came to him because of the word, he was offended. Those that fell in thorny places are the ones who received the word, but the things of the world were more important than the word of God and he bore no fruit for the Kingdom.

I hope you are one of the last group where seed was sown on good ground. They not only heard it, but received it into their hearts and bore much fruit, some as much as a hundred fold. Which of the four will you be?

We have discussed people and things to pray for as well as thoughts about how to give meaning to our individual prayer lives.

The final thing I will say we need to pray for is revival. I'm not talking about the one or two week revivals various churches have. These are good and should be encouraged. Many people have been saved in these revivals.

I'm talking about a nationwide, Spirit filled revival that will shake the devil and his demons like they haven't been shaken since Christ rose from the dead. We need local revivals and state revivals that will expand throughout our nation. Pray for this kind of revival. Will you pray that it will begin in you?

Jesus said in Luke 10:2, *"... The **harvest** truly is great, but the labourers are few: **pray** ye therefore the Lord of the **harvest**, that he would send forth labourers into his **harvest**."*

Maybe someday our posterity will call us one of the two greatest generations because like my parent's generation, we stood firm for the sake of our great country.

May God be with you and this great United States of America as we humbly submit to Him, pray, seek His face, and turn from our wicked ways.

ADDENDUM

In the Beginning ...

... the Word was with God and the Word was God. All things came into being by Him. (John 1: 1-3) Jesus, the Word, was with God at creation and was Himself a vital part of creation as *the Spirit of God moved over the surface of the waters.* (Genesis 1:2). God the Father, Son, and Holy Spirit were all present and active at creation. *Then God said, "Let Us make man in Our image.* (Genesis 1:26). So all three persons of the Trinity were present and active when man was created as a breathing, living human being. Imagine what it would be like to have all three of them with you when you took your first breath!

In creating mankind in Their image, They made him a spirit being, housed in a human body, and with a soul. No other living creature possesses a soul or is a spirit being able to commune with the Almighty. We were created this way so we could commune with and worship God. Then man broke that special relationship with God by sinning. God is perfect and could not commune with man as He had intended. Not only did Adam and Eve sin, but you and I have sinned.

For all have sinned and come short of the glory of God. (Romans 3:23) *and the wages of sin is death* ... (Romans 6:23a). This death is eternal separation from God in a real place called Hell, which was created for the devil and his angels. But God did not create man with a soul and spirit to spend a few years on earth and then spend eternity separated from the loving arms of God. ...*but the free gift of God is eternal life in Christ Jesus our Lord.* (Romans 6:23b). Although we have all sinned and deserve to spend eternity in hell, God has a better plan through and only through his only begotten Son, Jesus Christ.

Jesus left His place in heaven and came to earth as a baby human being to live a life free from sin so He could take our sins upon Himself and pay the penalty of our sins as the Lamb without blemish so we can have eternal life in the presence of God. We cannot imagine what it must have been like to leave His place in Glory to walk the earth as a man with all the temptations and hardships of mankind and then to die on a cross, crucified in a most horrible way, forsaken by those closest to him, to pay the penalty for the sins of all mankind.

But He did it! Why? Because He loves you and me. Jesus went through a terrible ordeal so we could have a loving relationship with God the Father, Son, and Holy Spirit.

Then he was raised from the dead. God gave Him His life again and freed Him from the bondage of sin and death. Forty days later He ascended to again be with God the Father. Then He sent the Holy Spirit to be not only with us, but in us so we could live victorious Christian lives.

Jesus paid the price, so the gift of eternal life is free to those who will repent and accept Jesus as the Son of God who died on the cross to save us from our sins and rose again. It's that simple. But it's not just a matter of believing that He physically died and rose again. We must turn from our sins (repent) and receive Him as our Savior and Lord. Receive Him as your Savior from an eternity in hell and make Him Lord of your life. ...*if you confess with your mouth Jesus as Lord, and believe in your heart that God raised Him from the dead, you shall be saved.* (Romans 10:9)

If you haven't done it before, do it now. Confess that you are a sinner; ask for forgiveness; tell Him that you want to change your thoughts and actions with His help and guidance; and ask Jesus to come into your heart to give you eternal life in heaven with God the Father and His Son, Jesus Christ.

If you have done this, you are saved for eternity. God, Jesus, and the Holy Spirit have come into your very being: *Do you not know that you are a temple of God, and that the Spirit of God dwells in you?* (I Corinthians 3:16). Jesus did no miracles until the Holy Spirit came upon Him when He was baptized. You and I cannot live a victorious life without the guidance of the Holy Spirit. Know that Jesus has saved you, the Holy Spirit will help you through this life, and you will spend eternity with God in heaven.

The initial act of salvation is a one-time event. But it's just the beginning of your walk with God the Father, Son, and Holy Spirit. If you have just received Christ as your Lord and Savior, you are a babe in Christ now. But God wants you to become a spiritually mature man, woman, or child in Him

I encourage you to find a church where you can grow in your spiritual walk. Begin to read and study your Bible. The four gospels of the New Testament are Matthew, Mark, Luke, and John. These are the writings of the life of Jesus from the vantage points of these four men. Acts of the Apostles tells about some of the activities of some of the apostles and disciples after Christ's death. The other New Testament books are letters written by apostles and other spiritual men of that time. I would suggest that you begin with the gospel of John, then Acts, then back to one of the other three gospels. You might then alternate between the gospels and the letters of the New Testament.

Pray and read spiritual books that will help you grow in your spiritual walk (I generally prefer non-fiction). Begin to associate with fellow Christians. You can be a witness to former non-Christian friends, but don't associate with them like you did before because continuing or renewing old relationships may pull you back down. Always be looking up and forward to what God has in store for you.

If you have any questions, contact a pastor, spiritual leader, or friend you know who is a committed Christian. Remember that they are not perfect and neither are you. But they can help you grow in your spiritual walk. The Lord will guide your steps, but you have to take them.